50 Premium Chocolate Recipes for Home

By: Kelly Johnson

Table of Contents

- Classic Chocolate Fondant
- Dark Chocolate Truffles
- Chocolate Lava Cake
- White Chocolate Raspberry Cheesecake
- Chocolate Mousse
- Salted Caramel Chocolate Tarts
- Mocha Chocolate Cupcakes
- Mint Chocolate Brownies
- Almond Chocolate Bark
- Chocolate Hazelnut Spread
- Chocolate Covered Strawberries
- Espresso Chocolate Cake
- Peanut Butter Chocolate Bars
- Chocolate Chip Pancakes
- Chocolate-Covered Pretzels
- Red Velvet Chocolate Cake
- Dark Chocolate Almond Clusters
- Chocolate Peanut Butter Pie
- Chocolate Coconut Macaroons
- Chocolate Mint Ice Cream
- Triple Chocolate Cookies
- Spiced Hot Chocolate
- Orange Chocolate Soufflé
- Chocolate Pecan Pie
- Vegan Chocolate Avocado Mousse
- White Chocolate Cranberry Cookies
- Chocolate Chia Pudding
- Raspberry Chocolate Ganache Tart
- Chocolate Espresso Mousse
- Chocolate Almond Cake
- Chocolate Dipped Marshmallows
- Chocolate Mint Brownies
- Caramel Chocolate Cheesecake
- Chocolate Coconut Smoothie
- Dark Chocolate Cherry Bark
- Hazelnut Chocolate Cake

- Chocolate Covered Caramel Apples
- Strawberry Chocolate Shortcake
- Chocolate Banana Bread
- Dark Chocolate Pudding
- Chocolate Bourbon Balls
- Chocolate Almond Milkshake
- Chocolate Peanut Butter Truffles
- Chocolate Orange Bundt Cake
- Raspberry Chocolate Trifle
- Chocolate-Covered Rice Crispy Treats
- S'mores Chocolate Bars
- Spicy Chocolate Chili
- Chocolate Fig Bars
- Chocolate Almond Croissants

Classic Chocolate Fondant

Ingredients:

- 1/2 cup unsalted butter
- 4 ounces dark chocolate (70% cocoa), chopped
- 1 cup powdered sugar
- 2 large eggs
- 2 large egg yolks
- 1 teaspoon vanilla extract
- 1/4 cup all-purpose flour
- A pinch of salt
- Butter and cocoa powder (for greasing ramekins)

Instructions:

1. **Preheat Oven**: Preheat your oven to 425°F (220°C). Grease 4 ramekins with butter and dust with cocoa powder, tapping out any excess.
2. **Melt Chocolate and Butter**: In a heatproof bowl over a pot of simmering water (double boiler method), melt the butter and chopped dark chocolate together, stirring until smooth. Remove from heat and let it cool slightly.
3. **Mix Dry Ingredients**: In a separate bowl, whisk together the powdered sugar, flour, and a pinch of salt.
4. **Combine Ingredients**: Add the eggs and egg yolks to the melted chocolate mixture, whisking to combine. Stir in the vanilla extract.
5. **Add Dry Ingredients**: Gently fold in the dry ingredients until just combined. Be careful not to overmix.
6. **Fill Ramekins**: Divide the batter evenly among the prepared ramekins.
7. **Bake**: Place the ramekins on a baking sheet and bake in the preheated oven for 12-14 minutes, or until the edges are set but the center is still soft and slightly jiggly.
8. **Serve**: Let the fondants cool in the ramekins for 1 minute. Carefully run a knife around the edges to loosen them, then invert onto plates.
9. **Optional Garnish**: Dust with powdered sugar, serve with a scoop of vanilla ice cream, or add fresh berries for an extra touch.

Enjoy your classic chocolate fondant with its deliciously gooey center!

Dark Chocolate Truffles

Ingredients:

- 8 ounces dark chocolate (70% cocoa), finely chopped
- 1/2 cup heavy cream
- 2 tablespoons unsalted butter
- 1 teaspoon vanilla extract
- Cocoa powder, chopped nuts, or melted chocolate (for coating)

Instructions:

1. **Heat Cream**: In a small saucepan over medium heat, bring the heavy cream to a simmer. Do not let it boil.
2. **Melt Chocolate**: Place the chopped dark chocolate in a heatproof bowl. Pour the hot cream over the chocolate and let it sit for 2-3 minutes to soften.
3. **Mix Ganache**: Stir the chocolate and cream mixture until smooth and fully combined. Add the unsalted butter and vanilla extract, stirring until the butter is melted and the ganache is glossy.
4. **Chill Ganache**: Cover the bowl with plastic wrap and refrigerate for about 1-2 hours, or until the ganache is firm enough to scoop.
5. **Form Truffles**: Once chilled, use a small cookie scoop or spoon to portion out the ganache. Roll the portions between your hands to form smooth balls.
6. **Coat Truffles**: Roll the truffles in your choice of coating:
    - **Cocoa Powder**: For a classic finish, roll the truffles in cocoa powder.
    - **Chopped Nuts**: Roll in finely chopped nuts for added texture.
    - **Melted Chocolate**: Dip the truffles in melted chocolate, then let them set on a parchment-lined tray.
7. **Chill Again**: Place the coated truffles on a baking sheet and refrigerate for an additional 30 minutes to set.
8. **Serve**: Enjoy your dark chocolate truffles as a luxurious treat, or package them as a thoughtful gift.

These truffles are rich, smooth, and perfect for any chocolate lover.

Chocolate Lava Cake

Ingredients:

- 1/2 cup unsalted butter (plus extra for greasing)
- 4 ounces dark chocolate (70% cocoa), chopped
- 1 cup powdered sugar
- 2 large eggs
- 2 large egg yolks
- 1 teaspoon vanilla extract
- 1/2 cup all-purpose flour
- A pinch of salt
- Butter and cocoa powder (for greasing ramekins)

Instructions:

1. **Preheat Oven**: Preheat your oven to 425°F (220°C). Grease 4 ramekins with butter and dust with cocoa powder, tapping out any excess.
2. **Melt Chocolate and Butter**: In a heatproof bowl over a pot of simmering water (double boiler method), melt the butter and chopped dark chocolate together, stirring until smooth. Remove from heat and let it cool slightly.
3. **Mix Dry Ingredients**: In a separate bowl, whisk together the powdered sugar, flour, and a pinch of salt.
4. **Combine Ingredients**: Add the eggs and egg yolks to the melted chocolate mixture, whisking to combine. Stir in the vanilla extract.
5. **Add Dry Ingredients**: Gently fold in the dry ingredients until just combined. Be careful not to overmix.
6. **Fill Ramekins**: Divide the batter evenly among the prepared ramekins.
7. **Bake**: Place the ramekins on a baking sheet and bake in the preheated oven for 12-14 minutes. The edges should be set, but the center will still be soft and slightly jiggly.
8. **Serve**: Let the cakes cool in the ramekins for 1 minute. Carefully run a knife around the edges to loosen them, then invert onto plates.
9. **Optional Garnishes**: Dust with powdered sugar, or serve with a scoop of vanilla ice cream or fresh berries for extra indulgence.

Enjoy the warm, molten center of your chocolate lava cakes!

White Chocolate Raspberry Cheesecake

Ingredients:

For the Crust:

- 1 1/2 cups graham cracker crumbs
- 1/4 cup granulated sugar
- 1/2 cup unsalted butter, melted

For the Filling:

- 8 ounces cream cheese, softened
- 1 cup white chocolate, chopped
- 1/2 cup sour cream
- 1/2 cup heavy cream
- 3/4 cup granulated sugar
- 3 large eggs
- 1 teaspoon vanilla extract
- 1 cup fresh or frozen raspberries (thawed and drained if using frozen)

For the Raspberry Swirl:

- 1/2 cup fresh or frozen raspberries
- 2 tablespoons granulated sugar

Instructions:

Prepare the Crust:

1. **Preheat Oven**: Preheat your oven to 325°F (163°C).
2. **Mix Crust**: In a medium bowl, combine the graham cracker crumbs, granulated sugar, and melted butter. Mix until the crumbs are evenly coated.
3. **Press Crust**: Press the mixture firmly into the bottom of a 9-inch springform pan to form an even layer. Bake for 10 minutes, then remove from the oven and let cool.

Prepare the Raspberry Swirl:

1. **Cook Raspberries**: In a small saucepan, cook the raspberries and granulated sugar over medium heat, stirring frequently until the raspberries break down and the mixture thickens (about 5-7 minutes).
2. **Cool Mixture**: Remove from heat and let it cool slightly.

Prepare the Filling:

1. **Melt Chocolate**: In a heatproof bowl over a pot of simmering water (double boiler method), melt the white chocolate until smooth. Let it cool slightly.
2. **Beat Cream Cheese**: In a large mixing bowl, beat the softened cream cheese until smooth and creamy.
3. **Add Ingredients**: Mix in the melted white chocolate, sour cream, heavy cream, and granulated sugar until well combined. Add the eggs, one at a time, beating on low speed after each addition. Stir in the vanilla extract.
4. **Add Raspberries**: Gently fold in the raspberries, being careful not to break them up too much.

Assemble and Bake:

1. **Pour Filling**: Pour the cheesecake filling over the cooled crust in the springform pan.
2. **Add Swirl**: Drop spoonfuls of the raspberry mixture onto the cheesecake filling. Use a knife or toothpick to swirl the raspberry mixture into the filling.
3. **Bake**: Bake in the preheated oven for 50-60 minutes, or until the center is set but still slightly jiggly.
4. **Cool**: Turn off the oven and let the cheesecake cool in the oven with the door slightly ajar for 1 hour. Then, refrigerate for at least 4 hours or overnight to set completely.

Serve:

1. **Remove from Pan**: Carefully remove the cheesecake from the springform pan.
2. **Garnish**: Optional: Garnish with extra fresh raspberries and a dusting of powdered sugar if desired.

Enjoy your creamy, delightful White Chocolate Raspberry Cheesecake!

Chocolate Mousse

Ingredients:

- 6 ounces dark chocolate (70% cocoa), chopped
- 2 tablespoons unsalted butter
- 3 large eggs, separated
- 1/4 cup granulated sugar
- 1/2 teaspoon vanilla extract
- 1 cup heavy cream
- A pinch of salt

Instructions:

1. **Melt Chocolate**:
   - In a heatproof bowl over a pot of simmering water (double boiler method), melt the dark chocolate and butter together, stirring until smooth. Remove from heat and let it cool slightly.
2. **Prepare Egg Yolks**:
   - In a separate bowl, whisk the egg yolks with granulated sugar until the mixture is thick and pale.
   - Stir the egg yolk mixture into the melted chocolate until fully combined. Add the vanilla extract and mix well.
3. **Beat Egg Whites**:
   - In a clean bowl, beat the egg whites with a pinch of salt using an electric mixer until stiff peaks form.
   - Gently fold the beaten egg whites into the chocolate mixture in three additions, being careful not to deflate them.
4. **Whip Cream**:
   - In another bowl, beat the heavy cream until soft peaks form.
   - Gently fold the whipped cream into the chocolate mixture until fully incorporated.
5. **Chill Mousse**:
   - Spoon the mousse into serving glasses or bowls.
   - Refrigerate for at least 2 hours, or until set.
6. **Serve**:
   - Garnish with shaved chocolate, berries, or a dollop of whipped cream if desired.

Enjoy your rich and creamy chocolate mousse!

Salted Caramel Chocolate Tarts

Ingredients:

For the Tart Crust:

- 1 1/2 cups all-purpose flour
- 1/4 cup granulated sugar
- 1/2 teaspoon salt
- 1/2 cup unsalted butter, chilled and cut into small pieces
- 1 large egg yolk
- 2 tablespoons cold water (more if needed)

For the Caramel Filling:

- 1 cup granulated sugar
- 6 tablespoons unsalted butter, cut into pieces
- 1/2 cup heavy cream
- 1/2 teaspoon sea salt

For the Chocolate Ganache:

- 8 ounces dark chocolate (70% cocoa), chopped
- 1 cup heavy cream
- 1 teaspoon vanilla extract

For Garnish:

- Sea salt flakes
- Whipped cream (optional)

Instructions:

Prepare the Tart Crust:

1. **Mix Dry Ingredients**: In a food processor, combine the flour, granulated sugar, and salt.
2. **Cut in Butter**: Add the chilled butter and pulse until the mixture resembles coarse crumbs.
3. **Add Egg Yolk**: Add the egg yolk and pulse until combined.
4. **Add Water**: Gradually add cold water, one tablespoon at a time, until the dough comes together.
5. **Chill Dough**: Turn the dough out onto a lightly floured surface, form it into a disk, wrap in plastic wrap, and refrigerate for at least 30 minutes.

Bake the Tart Crust:

1. **Preheat Oven**: Preheat your oven to 350°F (175°C).
2. **Roll Out Dough**: On a floured surface, roll out the dough to about 1/8-inch thickness. Cut to fit into tart pans.
3. **Fit into Pans**: Press the dough into the tart pans and trim any excess. Prick the bottom with a fork.
4. **Blind Bake**: Place a piece of parchment paper or foil over the dough and fill with pie weights or dried beans. Bake for 10 minutes, then remove the weights and parchment and bake for another 5 minutes, until golden brown. Let cool completely.

Prepare the Caramel Filling:

1. **Make Caramel**: In a medium saucepan over medium heat, melt the sugar until it becomes a golden amber color, stirring constantly.
2. **Add Butter**: Carefully add the butter and stir until melted and combined.
3. **Add Cream**: Slowly add the heavy cream while stirring. The mixture will bubble up, so be cautious.
4. **Season**: Stir in the sea salt. Let the caramel cool slightly before pouring it into the cooled tart crusts. Refrigerate to set.

Prepare the Chocolate Ganache:

1. **Heat Cream**: In a small saucepan, heat the heavy cream until it just begins to simmer.
2. **Add Chocolate**: Place the chopped dark chocolate in a heatproof bowl. Pour the hot cream over the chocolate and let it sit for 2-3 minutes.
3. **Mix Ganache**: Stir the mixture until smooth and glossy. Stir in the vanilla extract.
4. **Top Tarts**: Pour the ganache over the set caramel in each tart. Smooth the top with a spatula.

Garnish and Serve:

1. **Chill Tarts**: Refrigerate the tarts until the ganache is set, about 1 hour.
2. **Garnish**: Sprinkle sea salt flakes over the top of each tart. Optionally, serve with a dollop of whipped cream.

Enjoy your luxurious salted caramel chocolate tarts with their rich layers of flavor!

Mocha Chocolate Cupcakes

Ingredients:

For the Cupcakes:

- 1 cup all-purpose flour
- 1/2 cup unsweetened cocoa powder
- 1 cup granulated sugar
- 1/2 teaspoon baking powder
- 1/2 teaspoon baking soda
- 1/4 teaspoon salt
- 1/2 cup unsalted butter, room temperature
- 2 large eggs
- 1/2 cup strong brewed coffee (cooled)
- 1/2 cup whole milk
- 1 teaspoon vanilla extract

For the Mocha Frosting:

- 1/2 cup unsalted butter, room temperature
- 2 cups powdered sugar
- 1/4 cup unsweetened cocoa powder
- 1 tablespoon instant coffee granules
- 2-3 tablespoons milk or heavy cream
- 1 teaspoon vanilla extract

Instructions:

Prepare the Cupcakes:

1. **Preheat Oven**: Preheat your oven to 350°F (175°C) and line a 12-cup muffin tin with cupcake liners.
2. **Mix Dry Ingredients**: In a medium bowl, whisk together the flour, cocoa powder, sugar, baking powder, baking soda, and salt.
3. **Cream Butter**: In a large bowl, beat the butter until creamy using an electric mixer.
4. **Add Eggs**: Add the eggs one at a time, beating well after each addition.
5. **Combine Wet Ingredients**: Mix in the vanilla extract.
6. **Combine Dry and Wet**: Gradually add the dry ingredients to the butter mixture in three additions, alternating with the coffee and milk, beginning and ending with the dry ingredients. Mix until just combined.
7. **Fill and Bake**: Divide the batter evenly among the cupcake liners, filling each about 2/3 full. Bake for 18-20 minutes, or until a toothpick inserted into the center comes out clean.
8. **Cool**: Let the cupcakes cool in the tin for 5 minutes, then transfer to a wire rack to cool completely.

Prepare the Mocha Frosting:

1. **Dissolve Coffee**: In a small bowl, dissolve the instant coffee granules in 1 tablespoon of hot water.
2. **Beat Butter**: In a large bowl, beat the butter until creamy.
3. **Add Cocoa Powder**: Gradually mix in the powdered sugar and cocoa powder, beating on low speed until combined.
4. **Add Coffee and Milk**: Add the dissolved coffee, 2 tablespoons of milk, and vanilla extract. Beat until smooth and creamy. Add more milk if needed to achieve the desired consistency.

Frost the Cupcakes:

1. **Frost Cupcakes**: Once the cupcakes are completely cooled, frost with the mocha frosting using a piping bag or a knife.
2. **Optional Garnish**: Decorate with chocolate shavings or a light dusting of cocoa powder if desired.

Enjoy your Mocha Chocolate Cupcakes, perfect for any coffee and chocolate lover!

Mint Chocolate Brownies

Ingredients:

For the Brownies:

- 1/2 cup unsalted butter
- 4 ounces dark chocolate (70% cocoa), chopped
- 1 cup granulated sugar
- 2 large eggs
- 1 teaspoon vanilla extract
- 1/2 cup all-purpose flour
- 1/4 cup unsweetened cocoa powder
- 1/4 teaspoon salt
- 1/4 teaspoon baking powder

For the Mint Layer:

- 1/4 cup unsalted butter, room temperature
- 2 cups powdered sugar
- 2 tablespoons heavy cream
- 1/2 teaspoon peppermint extract (adjust to taste)
- A few drops of green food coloring (optional)

For the Chocolate Glaze:

- 4 ounces semisweet chocolate, chopped
- 2 tablespoons unsalted butter

Instructions:

Prepare the Brownies:

1. **Preheat Oven**: Preheat your oven to 350°F (175°C) and grease an 8x8-inch baking pan or line it with parchment paper.
2. **Melt Butter and Chocolate**: In a medium saucepan, melt the butter and chopped dark chocolate together over low heat, stirring until smooth. Remove from heat and let it cool slightly.
3. **Mix Sugar and Eggs**: Stir the granulated sugar into the melted chocolate mixture. Add the eggs, one at a time, beating well after each addition. Mix in the vanilla extract.
4. **Combine Dry Ingredients**: In a separate bowl, whisk together the flour, cocoa powder, salt, and baking powder.
5. **Combine Mixtures**: Gradually fold the dry ingredients into the chocolate mixture until just combined.

6. **Bake Brownies**: Pour the batter into the prepared pan and spread it evenly. Bake for 20-25 minutes, or until a toothpick inserted into the center comes out with a few moist crumbs. Let the brownies cool completely in the pan on a wire rack.

Prepare the Mint Layer:

1. **Beat Ingredients**: In a medium bowl, beat the butter until creamy. Gradually add the powdered sugar, heavy cream, and peppermint extract, beating until smooth. Add a few drops of green food coloring if desired.
2. **Spread Mint Layer**: Once the brownies are completely cooled, spread the mint layer evenly over the brownies.

Prepare the Chocolate Glaze:

1. **Melt Chocolate and Butter**: In a heatproof bowl over a pot of simmering water (double boiler method), melt the semisweet chocolate and butter together, stirring until smooth.
2. **Glaze Brownies**: Pour the chocolate glaze over the mint layer, spreading it evenly with a spatula.
3. **Chill and Cut**: Refrigerate the brownies for about 30 minutes, or until the chocolate glaze is set. Once set, cut into squares and serve.

Enjoy your Mint Chocolate Brownies with their perfect combination of rich chocolate and refreshing mint!

Almond Chocolate Bark

Ingredients:

- 12 ounces (340 grams) dark chocolate or semi-sweet chocolate, chopped
- 1/2 cup whole almonds (roasted or raw, but toasted if desired)
- 1/4 cup slivered almonds (for garnish)
- Sea salt (optional, for sprinkling)

Instructions:

1. **Prepare Baking Sheet**:
    - Line a baking sheet with parchment paper or a silicone baking mat.
2. **Melt Chocolate**:
    - In a heatproof bowl over a pot of simmering water (double boiler method), melt the chopped chocolate, stirring until smooth. Alternatively, melt the chocolate in the microwave in 20-second intervals, stirring after each interval, until fully melted and smooth.
3. **Mix in Almonds**:
    - Once the chocolate is melted, stir in the whole almonds until evenly coated.
4. **Spread Chocolate**:
    - Pour the chocolate mixture onto the prepared baking sheet and spread it out into an even layer with a spatula.
5. **Add Garnish**:
    - Sprinkle the slivered almonds over the top of the melted chocolate. Add a pinch of sea salt if using.
6. **Chill**:
    - Refrigerate the chocolate bark for about 30 minutes, or until it is completely set and firm.
7. **Break into Pieces**:
    - Once set, break the bark into pieces or shards.
8. **Store**:
    - Store the almond chocolate bark in an airtight container at room temperature or in the refrigerator.

Enjoy your crunchy, nutty, and richly flavored almond chocolate bark!

Chocolate Hazelnut Spread

Ingredients:

- 1 cup hazelnuts (roasted and peeled)
- 1/2 cup powdered sugar
- 1/2 cup cocoa powder
- 1/4 cup chocolate chips or chopped dark chocolate
- 1/4 cup milk (or a non-dairy alternative)
- 2 tablespoons unsalted butter (or coconut oil for a dairy-free version)
- 1 teaspoon vanilla extract
- A pinch of salt

Instructions:

1. **Prepare Hazelnuts**:
   - Preheat your oven to 350°F (175°C). Spread the hazelnuts in a single layer on a baking sheet and roast for 10-12 minutes, or until fragrant and the skins start to crack. Let them cool slightly, then rub the nuts with a kitchen towel to remove as much of the skins as possible. You can also use pre-roasted and peeled hazelnuts if available.
2. **Blend Hazelnuts**:
   - Place the hazelnuts in a food processor and blend until they turn into a smooth paste, scraping down the sides as needed. This may take a few minutes.
3. **Add Ingredients**:
   - Add the powdered sugar, cocoa powder, and a pinch of salt to the hazelnut paste. Blend until well combined.
4. **Melt Chocolate**:
   - In a heatproof bowl over a pot of simmering water (double boiler method), melt the chocolate chips or chopped dark chocolate with the butter (or coconut oil). Stir until smooth.
5. **Combine Mixtures**:
   - Add the melted chocolate mixture and vanilla extract to the hazelnut paste. Blend until smooth and fully combined.
6. **Add Milk**:
   - Gradually add the milk, blending until the mixture reaches your desired consistency. If it's too thick, you can add a bit more milk to achieve a smoother texture.
7. **Store**:
   - Transfer the spread to a clean jar or airtight container. Store at room temperature for up to 2 weeks or refrigerate for longer shelf life.

Enjoy your homemade chocolate hazelnut spread on toast, as a dip, or in your favorite recipes!

Chocolate Covered Strawberries

Ingredients:

- 1 pound (450 grams) fresh strawberries (preferably large and with stems)
- 8 ounces (225 grams) dark chocolate, semi-sweet chocolate, or milk chocolate, chopped
- 2 tablespoons coconut oil or vegetable oil (optional, for a smoother coating)
- 1/4 cup white chocolate or milk chocolate, for drizzling (optional)

Instructions:

1. **Prepare Strawberries**:
   - Wash the strawberries and pat them dry with paper towels. Ensure they are completely dry before dipping, as water can cause the chocolate to seize.
2. **Melt Chocolate**:
   - **Double Boiler Method**: Place the chopped chocolate and coconut oil (if using) in a heatproof bowl over a pot of simmering water. Stir until the chocolate is fully melted and smooth.
   - **Microwave Method**: Place the chopped chocolate and coconut oil (if using) in a microwave-safe bowl. Microwave in 20-second intervals, stirring after each interval, until the chocolate is completely melted and smooth.
3. **Dip Strawberries**:
   - Hold each strawberry by the stem and dip it into the melted chocolate, covering about two-thirds of the strawberry. Allow any excess chocolate to drip off.
4. **Set Chocolate**:
   - Place the dipped strawberries on a baking sheet lined with parchment paper or a silicone mat. Refrigerate for about 15-30 minutes, or until the chocolate is set.
5. **Optional Drizzle**:
   - If desired, melt the white chocolate or additional milk chocolate as described above. Use a fork or a piping bag to drizzle the melted chocolate over the set dark chocolate layer for an added decorative touch.
6. **Serve and Store**:
   - Serve the chocolate-covered strawberries immediately or store them in the refrigerator for up to 2 days. They are best enjoyed fresh.

These chocolate-covered strawberries are perfect for sharing or gifting, offering a delicious combination of juicy strawberries and rich chocolate!

Espresso Chocolate Cake

Ingredients:

For the Cake:

- 1 3/4 cups all-purpose flour
- 1 1/2 cups granulated sugar
- 3/4 cup unsweetened cocoa powder
- 1 1/2 teaspoons baking powder
- 1 1/2 teaspoons baking soda
- 1/2 teaspoon salt
- 1 cup hot brewed espresso or strong coffee (cooled slightly)
- 1/2 cup buttermilk
- 1/2 cup vegetable oil
- 2 large eggs
- 2 teaspoons vanilla extract

For the Espresso Chocolate Ganache:

- 8 ounces dark chocolate, chopped
- 1/2 cup heavy cream
- 1 tablespoon brewed espresso or strong coffee
- 1 tablespoon unsalted butter

Instructions:

Prepare the Cake:

1. **Preheat Oven**: Preheat your oven to 350°F (175°C). Grease and flour two 8-inch round cake pans, or line them with parchment paper.
2. **Mix Dry Ingredients**: In a large bowl, whisk together the flour, sugar, cocoa powder, baking powder, baking soda, and salt.
3. **Combine Wet Ingredients**: In another bowl, mix together the hot espresso or coffee, buttermilk, vegetable oil, eggs, and vanilla extract.
4. **Combine Mixtures**: Gradually add the wet ingredients to the dry ingredients, mixing until just combined. Be careful not to overmix.
5. **Bake**: Divide the batter evenly between the prepared cake pans. Bake for 25-30 minutes, or until a toothpick inserted into the center comes out clean.
6. **Cool**: Let the cakes cool in the pans for 10 minutes, then transfer to wire racks to cool completely.

Prepare the Espresso Chocolate Ganache:

1. **Heat Cream**: In a small saucepan, heat the heavy cream until it just begins to simmer.

2. **Melt Chocolate**: Place the chopped dark chocolate in a heatproof bowl. Pour the hot cream over the chocolate and let it sit for 2-3 minutes.
3. **Mix Ganache**: Stir the chocolate and cream mixture until smooth. Add the brewed espresso and butter, stirring until fully incorporated and smooth.
4. **Cool Ganache**: Let the ganache cool slightly until it thickens to a spreadable consistency.

Assemble the Cake:

1. **Frost Cake**: Place one layer of the cake on a serving plate. Spread a layer of ganache on top. Place the second cake layer on top and spread the remaining ganache over the top and sides of the cake.
2. **Decorate**: Optionally, garnish with chocolate shavings, espresso beans, or a dusting of cocoa powder.
3. **Serve**: Let the cake set for about 30 minutes before slicing to allow the ganache to firm up.

Enjoy your rich and indulgent Espresso Chocolate Cake, perfect for any chocolate and coffee lover!

Peanut Butter Chocolate Bars

Ingredients:

For the Peanut Butter Layer:

- 1 cup creamy peanut butter
- 1/2 cup unsalted butter
- 2 cups graham cracker crumbs
- 2 cups powdered sugar

For the Chocolate Topping:

- 1 cup semisweet chocolate chips
- 1/4 cup creamy peanut butter

Instructions:

Prepare the Peanut Butter Layer:

1. **Melt Butter and Peanut Butter**: In a medium saucepan over low heat, melt the butter and peanut butter together, stirring until smooth and fully combined.
2. **Combine with Crumbs and Sugar**: Remove from heat and stir in the graham cracker crumbs and powdered sugar until well mixed.
3. **Press into Pan**: Press the peanut butter mixture evenly into the bottom of a greased 9x13-inch baking pan or one lined with parchment paper.
4. **Chill**: Refrigerate the peanut butter layer while you prepare the chocolate topping.

Prepare the Chocolate Topping:

1. **Melt Chocolate and Peanut Butter**: In a microwave-safe bowl, combine the chocolate chips and 1/4 cup peanut butter. Microwave in 20-second intervals, stirring after each, until the mixture is smooth and fully melted. You can also melt this mixture in a heatproof bowl over a pot of simmering water.
2. **Spread Chocolate**: Pour the melted chocolate mixture over the chilled peanut butter layer. Use a spatula to spread it evenly.
3. **Chill Again**: Refrigerate for at least 1 hour, or until the chocolate topping is set.

Serve:

1. **Cut Bars**: Once set, remove from the pan and cut into bars or squares.
2. **Store**: Store the bars in an airtight container in the refrigerator for up to 2 weeks.

These Peanut Butter Chocolate Bars are perfect for a sweet treat or a party snack, offering a delightful combination of flavors and textures!

Chocolate Chip Pancakes

Ingredients:

For the Pancakes:

- 1 1/2 cups all-purpose flour
- 2 tablespoons granulated sugar
- 1 tablespoon baking powder
- 1/2 teaspoon salt
- 1 cup milk (whole or 2% for best results)
- 1/4 cup melted butter or vegetable oil
- 1 large egg
- 1 teaspoon vanilla extract
- 1/2 cup chocolate chips (semi-sweet or milk chocolate)

Instructions:

1. **Prepare Dry Ingredients**:
    - In a large bowl, whisk together the flour, sugar, baking powder, and salt.
2. **Prepare Wet Ingredients**:
    - In another bowl, whisk together the milk, melted butter (or oil), egg, and vanilla extract.
3. **Combine Mixtures**:
    - Pour the wet ingredients into the dry ingredients and stir gently until just combined. The batter may be a bit lumpy, and that's okay. Be careful not to overmix.
4. **Fold in Chocolate Chips**:
    - Gently fold the chocolate chips into the batter.
5. **Preheat Griddle/Pan**:
    - Heat a griddle or large skillet over medium heat. Lightly grease with butter or cooking spray.
6. **Cook Pancakes**:
    - For each pancake, pour about 1/4 cup of batter onto the hot griddle or skillet. Cook until bubbles form on the surface of the pancake and the edges look set, about 2-3 minutes. Flip and cook for an additional 1-2 minutes, or until golden brown and cooked through.
7. **Serve**:
    - Serve warm with your favorite toppings such as maple syrup, additional chocolate chips, whipped cream, or fresh fruit.

Enjoy your fluffy and chocolatey pancakes, perfect for a sweet breakfast or brunch!

Chocolate-Covered Pretzels

Ingredients:

- 1 cup pretzel rods or pretzel twists
- 1 cup semi-sweet chocolate chips or chopped dark chocolate
- 1/2 cup white chocolate chips (optional, for drizzling)
- Sprinkles, crushed nuts, or sea salt (optional, for garnish)

Instructions:

1. **Prepare Pretzels**:
    - Line a baking sheet with parchment paper or a silicone baking mat. This will prevent the pretzels from sticking and make cleanup easier.
2. **Melt Chocolate**:
    - **Double Boiler Method**: In a heatproof bowl over a pot of simmering water, melt the semi-sweet chocolate chips, stirring until smooth. Remove from heat and let it cool slightly.
    - **Microwave Method**: Place the semi-sweet chocolate chips in a microwave-safe bowl. Microwave in 20-second intervals, stirring after each interval, until melted and smooth.
3. **Dip Pretzels**:
    - Hold each pretzel by one end and dip it into the melted chocolate, covering about two-thirds of the pretzel. Allow excess chocolate to drip off.
4. **Add Garnishes** (Optional):
    - If desired, immediately sprinkle the dipped pretzels with toppings like sprinkles, crushed nuts, or a pinch of sea salt before the chocolate sets.
5. **Drizzle with White Chocolate** (Optional):
    - Melt the white chocolate chips using the same method as the semi-sweet chocolate. Once melted, drizzle over the dipped pretzels using a fork or a piping bag for a decorative touch.
6. **Set Chocolate**:
    - Place the dipped pretzels on the prepared baking sheet. Refrigerate for about 15-20 minutes, or until the chocolate is completely set.
7. **Store**:
    - Store the chocolate-covered pretzels in an airtight container at room temperature or in the refrigerator.

Enjoy your crunchy, sweet, and salty chocolate-covered pretzels!

Red Velvet Chocolate Cake

Ingredients:

For the Cake:

- 2 1/2 cups all-purpose flour
- 1 1/2 cups granulated sugar
- 1/2 cup unsweetened cocoa powder
- 1 teaspoon baking powder
- 1 teaspoon baking soda
- 1/2 teaspoon salt
- 1 cup vegetable oil
- 1 cup buttermilk
- 2 large eggs
- 2 tablespoons red food coloring
- 1 tablespoon white vinegar
- 1 teaspoon vanilla extract

For the Cream Cheese Frosting:

- 1/2 cup unsalted butter, room temperature
- 8 ounces cream cheese, room temperature
- 4 cups powdered sugar
- 1 teaspoon vanilla extract

Instructions:

Prepare the Cake:

1. **Preheat Oven**: Preheat your oven to 350°F (175°C). Grease and flour two 9-inch round cake pans or line them with parchment paper.
2. **Mix Dry Ingredients**: In a large bowl, sift together the flour, sugar, cocoa powder, baking powder, baking soda, and salt.
3. **Combine Wet Ingredients**: In another bowl, whisk together the oil, buttermilk, eggs, food coloring, vinegar, and vanilla extract.
4. **Combine Mixtures**: Gradually add the wet ingredients to the dry ingredients, mixing until just combined. Be careful not to overmix.
5. **Bake**: Divide the batter evenly between the prepared cake pans. Bake for 25-30 minutes, or until a toothpick inserted into the center comes out clean.
6. **Cool**: Let the cakes cool in the pans for 10 minutes, then transfer them to wire racks to cool completely.

Prepare the Cream Cheese Frosting:

1. **Beat Butter and Cream Cheese**: In a large bowl, beat the butter and cream cheese together until smooth and creamy.
2. **Add Powdered Sugar and Vanilla**: Gradually add the powdered sugar, beating on low speed until combined. Increase the speed and beat until light and fluffy. Mix in the vanilla extract.

Assemble the Cake:

1. **Frost Cake**: Place one cake layer on a serving plate. Spread a layer of cream cheese frosting over the top. Place the second cake layer on top and frost the top and sides of the cake with the remaining cream cheese frosting.
2. **Decorate**: Optionally, garnish with additional decorations such as sprinkles, chocolate shavings, or red velvet cake crumbs.
3. **Serve**: Allow the cake to set for about 30 minutes before slicing to make sure the frosting is well-set.

Enjoy your vibrant and indulgent Red Velvet Chocolate Cake, perfect for special occasions or as a treat for any day!

Dark Chocolate Almond Clusters

Ingredients:

- 1 cup whole almonds (roasted or raw, but toasted for extra flavor)
- 8 ounces dark chocolate (70% cocoa or your preferred variety), chopped
- 1/2 teaspoon sea salt (optional, for sprinkling)

Instructions:

1. **Prepare Baking Sheet**:
    - Line a baking sheet with parchment paper or a silicone baking mat. This will prevent the clusters from sticking and make cleanup easier.
2. **Toast Almonds** (if using raw):
    - Preheat your oven to 350°F (175°C). Spread the almonds in a single layer on a baking sheet and toast for 8-10 minutes, or until fragrant and lightly golden. Let them cool completely.
3. **Melt Chocolate**:
    - **Double Boiler Method**: Place the chopped dark chocolate in a heatproof bowl over a pot of simmering water. Stir until melted and smooth.
    - **Microwave Method**: Place the chopped chocolate in a microwave-safe bowl. Microwave in 20-second intervals, stirring after each interval, until the chocolate is fully melted and smooth.
4. **Combine Almonds and Chocolate**:
    - Stir the almonds into the melted chocolate until they are fully coated.
5. **Form Clusters**:
    - Drop spoonfuls of the chocolate-almond mixture onto the prepared baking sheet, forming clusters of your desired size.
6. **Add Sea Salt** (optional):
    - If desired, lightly sprinkle a pinch of sea salt over each cluster before the chocolate sets.
7. **Set Chocolate**:
    - Refrigerate the clusters for about 15-20 minutes, or until the chocolate is completely set.
8. **Store**:
    - Store the dark chocolate almond clusters in an airtight container at room temperature or in the refrigerator. They should keep well for up to 2 weeks.

Enjoy these crunchy, chocolatey clusters as a satisfying snack or a delightful treat for sharing!

Chocolate Peanut Butter Pie

Ingredients:

For the Crust:

- 1 1/2 cups chocolate cookie crumbs (such as Oreos or chocolate graham crackers)
- 1/4 cup granulated sugar
- 6 tablespoons unsalted butter, melted

For the Peanut Butter Filling:

- 1 cup creamy peanut butter
- 1 cup powdered sugar
- 1 cup heavy cream
- 1 teaspoon vanilla extract
- 4 ounces cream cheese, softened

For the Chocolate Ganache:

- 1 cup semisweet chocolate chips or chopped semisweet chocolate
- 1/2 cup heavy cream

For Garnish (Optional):

- Whipped cream
- Chopped peanuts
- Shaved chocolate

Instructions:

Prepare the Crust:

1. **Mix Crust Ingredients**: In a medium bowl, combine the chocolate cookie crumbs, granulated sugar, and melted butter. Stir until the mixture resembles wet sand.
2. **Press into Pan**: Press the crumb mixture evenly into the bottom and up the sides of a 9-inch pie pan.
3. **Bake**: Preheat your oven to 350°F (175°C). Bake the crust for 8-10 minutes. Remove from the oven and let it cool completely.

Prepare the Peanut Butter Filling:

1. **Beat Peanut Butter and Cream Cheese**: In a large bowl, beat the peanut butter and softened cream cheese together until smooth and creamy.
2. **Add Powdered Sugar and Vanilla**: Gradually add the powdered sugar and vanilla extract, beating until well combined.

3. **Whip Cream**: In a separate bowl, whip the heavy cream until stiff peaks form.
4. **Fold in Whipped Cream**: Gently fold the whipped cream into the peanut butter mixture until fully combined and smooth.
5. **Fill the Crust**: Spread the peanut butter filling evenly over the cooled chocolate crust.
6. **Chill**: Refrigerate the pie for at least 2 hours to set.

Prepare the Chocolate Ganache:

1. **Heat Cream**: In a small saucepan, heat the heavy cream until it just begins to simmer.
2. **Melt Chocolate**: Place the chocolate chips or chopped chocolate in a heatproof bowl. Pour the hot cream over the chocolate and let it sit for 2-3 minutes.
3. **Mix Ganache**: Stir the chocolate and cream mixture until smooth and fully combined.
4. **Cool Ganache**: Allow the ganache to cool slightly before spreading it over the peanut butter filling.

Assemble the Pie:

1. **Add Ganache**: Once the peanut butter filling is set, spread the chocolate ganache evenly over the top.
2. **Chill Again**: Refrigerate the pie for an additional 30 minutes to 1 hour, or until the ganache is firm.
3. **Garnish and Serve**: Optionally, top with whipped cream, chopped peanuts, or shaved chocolate before serving.

Enjoy your creamy, chocolatey, and peanut buttery pie!

Chocolate Coconut Macaroons

Ingredients:

For the Macaroons:

- 2 cups sweetened shredded coconut
- 1/2 cup granulated sugar
- 1/4 cup all-purpose flour
- 1/4 teaspoon salt
- 3 large egg whites
- 1 teaspoon vanilla extract

For the Chocolate Coating:

- 1 cup semi-sweet chocolate chips or chopped dark chocolate
- 2 tablespoons coconut oil (optional, for a smoother coating)

Instructions:

Prepare the Macaroons:

1. **Preheat Oven**: Preheat your oven to 325°F (165°C). Line a baking sheet with parchment paper or a silicone baking mat.
2. **Mix Dry Ingredients**: In a large bowl, combine the shredded coconut, granulated sugar, flour, and salt.
3. **Whisk Egg Whites**: In another bowl, whisk the egg whites until they form soft peaks. This means the egg whites should be slightly foamy and hold a shape when you lift the whisk.
4. **Combine Ingredients**: Gently fold the egg whites and vanilla extract into the coconut mixture until well combined. Be careful not to deflate the egg whites too much.
5. **Shape Macaroons**: Use a small cookie scoop or spoon to form the coconut mixture into mounds on the prepared baking sheet. Space them about 1 inch apart.
6. **Bake**: Bake for 15-20 minutes, or until the macaroons are golden brown. Allow them to cool completely on the baking sheet.

Prepare the Chocolate Coating:

1. **Melt Chocolate**: In a heatproof bowl over a pot of simmering water (double boiler method), melt the chocolate chips or chopped chocolate with the coconut oil (if using) until smooth. Alternatively, melt in the microwave in 20-second intervals, stirring after each interval.
2. **Dip Macaroons**: Once the macaroons are completely cooled, dip the bottom half of each macaroon into the melted chocolate, allowing excess chocolate to drip off.

3. **Set Chocolate**: Place the dipped macaroons back on the parchment-lined baking sheet. Refrigerate or let them sit at room temperature until the chocolate is fully set.

Serve and Store:

1. **Serve**: Enjoy your macaroons once the chocolate has hardened.
2. **Store**: Store the macaroons in an airtight container at room temperature or in the refrigerator for up to 1 week.

These Chocolate Coconut Macaroons are a delightful combination of chewy coconut and rich chocolate, perfect for satisfying your sweet tooth!

Chocolate Mint Ice Cream

Ingredients:

For the Mint Base:

- 1 cup whole milk
- 1 cup heavy cream
- 3/4 cup granulated sugar
- 1/2 cup packed fresh mint leaves (or 1 teaspoon peppermint extract)
- 4 large egg yolks

For the Chocolate Swirl:

- 1/2 cup semi-sweet chocolate chips or chopped dark chocolate
- 1/4 cup heavy cream

Instructions:

Prepare the Mint Base:

1. **Infuse Mint**: In a medium saucepan, combine the milk, heavy cream, and sugar. Heat over medium heat until the mixture is hot but not boiling. Remove from heat and add the fresh mint leaves. Let it steep for about 10 minutes. If using peppermint extract, skip this step and add it later.
2. **Strain Mint**: Strain the mint leaves from the mixture using a fine-mesh sieve or cheesecloth. Discard the mint leaves.
3. **Temper Egg Yolks**: In a separate bowl, whisk the egg yolks. Slowly add a small amount of the hot milk mixture to the egg yolks, whisking constantly to temper them. Gradually add the egg yolk mixture back into the saucepan with the remaining milk mixture, whisking continuously.
4. **Cook Custard**: Return the saucepan to the stove and cook over medium heat, stirring constantly, until the mixture thickens and coats the back of a spoon. This should take about 5-7 minutes.
5. **Cool Custard**: Remove from heat and let the custard cool to room temperature. If using peppermint extract, stir it in now.
6. **Chill**: Cover the custard with plastic wrap (pressing the wrap directly onto the surface to prevent a skin from forming) and refrigerate for at least 4 hours or overnight, until completely chilled.

Prepare the Chocolate Swirl:

1. **Heat Cream**: In a small saucepan, heat the heavy cream until it begins to simmer.

2. **Melt Chocolate**: Place the chocolate chips or chopped chocolate in a heatproof bowl. Pour the hot cream over the chocolate and let it sit for a minute. Stir until smooth and fully combined.
3. **Cool Chocolate**: Allow the chocolate ganache to cool slightly before swirling it into the ice cream.

Churn and Swirl:

1. **Churn Ice Cream**: Pour the chilled custard into an ice cream maker and churn according to the manufacturer's instructions, usually for about 20-25 minutes.
2. **Add Chocolate Swirl**: During the last few minutes of churning, slowly drizzle in the cooled chocolate ganache to create a swirl effect. Alternatively, you can fold the ganache into the churned ice cream once it's transferred to a storage container.
3. **Freeze**: Transfer the ice cream to an airtight container and freeze for at least 2 hours, or until firm.

Serve:

- Scoop and enjoy your homemade Chocolate Mint Ice Cream, perfect for a refreshing and indulgent dessert!

This ice cream combines the rich taste of chocolate with a cool, minty freshness, making it a delightful treat for any time of year.

Triple Chocolate Cookies

Ingredients:

- 1 cup unsalted butter, softened
- 1 cup granulated sugar
- 1 cup packed brown sugar
- 2 large eggs
- 1 teaspoon vanilla extract
- 2 1/4 cups all-purpose flour
- 1/2 cup unsweetened cocoa powder
- 1 teaspoon baking soda
- 1/2 teaspoon salt
- 1 cup semisweet chocolate chips
- 1/2 cup milk chocolate chips
- 1/2 cup white chocolate chips

Instructions:

1. **Preheat Oven**:
    - Preheat your oven to 350°F (175°C). Line a baking sheet with parchment paper or a silicone baking mat.
2. **Cream Butter and Sugars**:
    - In a large bowl, beat the softened butter, granulated sugar, and brown sugar together until light and fluffy.
3. **Add Eggs and Vanilla**:
    - Beat in the eggs one at a time, ensuring each is fully incorporated. Mix in the vanilla extract.
4. **Mix Dry Ingredients**:
    - In a separate bowl, whisk together the flour, cocoa powder, baking soda, and salt.
5. **Combine Mixtures**:
    - Gradually add the dry ingredients to the wet ingredients, mixing until just combined.
6. **Add Chocolate Chips**:
    - Fold in the semisweet chocolate chips, milk chocolate chips, and white chocolate chips.
7. **Scoop Cookies**:
    - Use a cookie scoop or tablespoon to drop rounded balls of dough onto the prepared baking sheet, spacing them about 2 inches apart.
8. **Bake**:
    - Bake for 10-12 minutes, or until the edges are set but the centers are still soft. The cookies will continue to cook slightly on the baking sheet after removing from the oven.
9. **Cool**:

- Allow the cookies to cool on the baking sheet for a few minutes before transferring them to a wire rack to cool completely.

Tips:

- **Chill the Dough**: For thicker cookies, chill the dough in the refrigerator for 30 minutes before baking.
- **Mix and Match**: Feel free to use different types of chocolate or add nuts for additional flavor and texture.

Enjoy these rich and gooey Triple Chocolate Cookies as a perfect treat for any chocolate lover!

Spiced Hot Chocolate

Ingredients:

- 2 cups whole milk (or any milk of your choice)
- 1/2 cup heavy cream
- 1/2 cup semi-sweet chocolate chips or chopped dark chocolate
- 2 tablespoons cocoa powder
- 1/4 cup granulated sugar (adjust to taste)
- 1/2 teaspoon ground cinnamon
- 1/4 teaspoon ground nutmeg
- 1/4 teaspoon ground allspice
- 1/4 teaspoon vanilla extract
- Pinch of salt

Optional Toppings:

- Whipped cream
- Marshmallows
- Chocolate shavings
- Ground cinnamon or nutmeg

Instructions:

1. **Heat Milk and Cream**:
   - In a medium saucepan, combine the milk and heavy cream. Heat over medium heat until the mixture is hot but not boiling.
2. **Mix Cocoa and Sugar**:
   - In a small bowl, mix the cocoa powder, granulated sugar, cinnamon, nutmeg, allspice, and a pinch of salt.
3. **Combine Chocolate and Spices**:
   - Add the cocoa mixture to the hot milk and cream, stirring until fully dissolved.
4. **Add Chocolate**:
   - Stir in the semi-sweet chocolate chips or chopped dark chocolate. Continue to stir until the chocolate is completely melted and the mixture is smooth.
5. **Add Vanilla**:
   - Remove from heat and stir in the vanilla extract.
6. **Serve**:
   - Pour the hot chocolate into mugs. Top with whipped cream, marshmallows, chocolate shavings, or a sprinkle of cinnamon or nutmeg if desired.
7. **Enjoy**:
   - Serve immediately and enjoy the rich, spiced flavor of your homemade hot chocolate!

This spiced hot chocolate is sure to be a hit with its warm, comforting spices and creamy chocolate flavor. Perfect for cozying up on a cold day or as a treat during the holiday season!

Orange Chocolate Soufflé

Ingredients:

For the Soufflé Base:

- 2 tablespoons unsalted butter, plus more for greasing
- 1/2 cup granulated sugar, plus extra for coating
- 4 ounces dark chocolate (70% cocoa), chopped
- 1 tablespoon all-purpose flour
- 1/2 cup whole milk
- 1 large egg yolk
- 2 large egg whites
- 1/4 teaspoon cream of tartar (optional, for stabilizing egg whites)
- Zest of 1 medium orange
- 1 tablespoon freshly squeezed orange juice
- 1/2 teaspoon vanilla extract
- Pinch of salt

For Serving (Optional):

- Powdered sugar, for dusting
- Whipped cream or vanilla ice cream

Instructions:

Prepare Soufflé Dishes:

1. **Preheat Oven**: Preheat your oven to 375°F (190°C).
2. **Prepare Dishes**: Grease four 6-ounce soufflé dishes or ramekins with unsalted butter. Dust the insides with granulated sugar, shaking out the excess. This helps the soufflés rise evenly.

Make the Chocolate Base:

1. **Melt Chocolate**: In a heatproof bowl, melt the dark chocolate over a pot of simmering water (double boiler method) or in the microwave in 20-second intervals, stirring until smooth. Let it cool slightly.
2. **Prepare Flour Mixture**: In a small saucepan, melt 2 tablespoons of butter over medium heat. Stir in the flour and cook for about 1 minute, until it forms a paste (roux). Gradually whisk in the milk and cook until the mixture is thickened and smooth.
3. **Combine with Chocolate**: Remove from heat and stir in the melted chocolate. Mix until fully combined. Let this mixture cool slightly.
4. **Add Egg Yolk**: Stir in the egg yolk, orange zest, orange juice, and vanilla extract. Mix until smooth.

Prepare Egg Whites:

1. **Beat Egg Whites**: In a clean, dry bowl, beat the egg whites with a pinch of salt (and cream of tartar, if using) until soft peaks form.
2. **Fold in Egg Whites**: Gently fold the beaten egg whites into the chocolate mixture in thirds. Be careful not to deflate the mixture. Fold until just combined, and no white streaks remain.

Bake:

1. **Fill Dishes**: Spoon the soufflé mixture into the prepared soufflé dishes, filling them almost to the top.
2. **Bake**: Place the dishes on a baking sheet and bake for 12-15 minutes, or until the soufflés have risen and are set in the middle. The tops should be slightly cracked.

Serve:

1. **Dust with Powdered Sugar**: Dust the soufflés with powdered sugar, if desired.
2. **Garnish**: Serve immediately with a dollop of whipped cream or a scoop of vanilla ice cream, if desired.

Tips:

- **Serve Immediately**: Soufflés should be served right out of the oven as they can deflate quickly.
- **Prep Ahead**: You can prepare the base ahead of time and refrigerate it. When ready to bake, bring it back to room temperature, fold in the egg whites, and bake.

Enjoy your elegant and delicious Orange Chocolate Soufflé!

Chocolate Pecan Pie

Ingredients:

For the Crust:

- 1 1/2 cups all-purpose flour
- 1/2 cup unsalted butter, chilled and cut into small cubes
- 1/4 cup granulated sugar
- 1/4 teaspoon salt
- 1/4 cup ice water (more if needed)

For the Filling:

- 1 cup chopped pecans
- 1 cup semi-sweet chocolate chips or chopped dark chocolate
- 1 cup light corn syrup
- 1/2 cup granulated sugar
- 1/4 cup packed brown sugar
- 1/4 cup unsalted butter, melted
- 3 large eggs
- 1 teaspoon vanilla extract
- 1/2 teaspoon salt

Instructions:

Prepare the Crust:

1. **Preheat Oven**: Preheat your oven to 350°F (175°C).
2. **Mix Crust Ingredients**: In a large bowl, combine the flour, sugar, and salt. Cut in the chilled butter using a pastry cutter or your fingers until the mixture resembles coarse crumbs.
3. **Add Water**: Gradually add ice water, 1 tablespoon at a time, mixing until the dough begins to come together. You may need a little more or less water, so add it slowly.
4. **Form and Chill**: Gather the dough into a ball, flatten it into a disc, and wrap it in plastic wrap. Refrigerate for at least 30 minutes.
5. **Roll Out Dough**: On a lightly floured surface, roll out the dough to fit a 9-inch pie dish. Transfer the dough to the dish, trim the edges, and crimp them as desired. Place the pie crust in the refrigerator while you prepare the filling.

Prepare the Filling:

1. **Preheat Oven**: Ensure your oven is still preheated to 350°F (175°C).
2. **Toast Pecans**: Toast the chopped pecans in a dry skillet over medium heat for about 3-5 minutes, until fragrant. Set aside to cool.

3. **Melt Chocolate**: In a heatproof bowl over a pot of simmering water (double boiler method) or in the microwave, melt the chocolate until smooth. Let it cool slightly.
4. **Mix Filling Ingredients**: In a large bowl, whisk together the corn syrup, granulated sugar, brown sugar, melted butter, eggs, vanilla extract, and salt. Stir in the melted chocolate until well combined.
5. **Add Pecans**: Gently fold in the toasted pecans.

Assemble and Bake:

1. **Fill Crust**: Pour the chocolate pecan filling into the prepared pie crust.
2. **Bake**: Bake for 50-60 minutes, or until the filling is set and the top is golden brown. The center should be slightly jiggly but will firm up as it cools.
3. **Cool**: Allow the pie to cool completely on a wire rack before slicing. This will help the filling set properly.

Serve:

- Serve at room temperature or slightly warmed. You can top it with whipped cream or a scoop of vanilla ice cream for extra indulgence.

Tips:

- **Check for Doneness**: If the crust starts to brown too quickly, cover the edges with foil to prevent burning.
- **Cool Completely**: Allow the pie to cool completely to help the filling set and slice cleanly.

Enjoy your rich and delicious Chocolate Pecan Pie, perfect for any special occasion or as a delightful treat!

Vegan Chocolate Avocado Mousse

Ingredients:

- 2 ripe avocados
- 1/4 cup unsweetened cocoa powder
- 1/4 cup pure maple syrup (or agave nectar)
- 1/4 cup coconut milk (or any plant-based milk)
- 1 teaspoon vanilla extract
- A pinch of sea salt
- Optional toppings: fresh berries, shredded coconut, or a sprinkle of sea salt

Instructions:

1. **Prepare Avocados:** Cut the avocados in half, remove the pit, and scoop the flesh into a food processor or blender.
2. **Blend Ingredients:** Add the cocoa powder, maple syrup, coconut milk, vanilla extract, and a pinch of sea salt to the avocados. Blend until smooth and creamy, scraping down the sides of the bowl as needed to ensure everything is well combined.
3. **Adjust Sweetness:** Taste the mousse and adjust the sweetness or cocoa powder according to your preference. Blend again if needed.
4. **Chill:** Transfer the mousse to serving bowls or glasses and refrigerate for at least 30 minutes to allow it to firm up and chill.
5. **Serve:** Before serving, add your choice of toppings such as fresh berries, shredded coconut, or a light sprinkle of sea salt.

Enjoy your rich, creamy, and healthy vegan chocolate avocado mousse!

White Chocolate Cranberry Cookies

Ingredients:

- 1 cup (2 sticks) unsalted butter, room temperature
- 1 cup granulated sugar
- 1 cup packed brown sugar
- 2 large eggs
- 1 teaspoon vanilla extract
- 3 cups all-purpose flour
- 1 teaspoon baking soda
- 1/2 teaspoon baking powder
- 1/2 teaspoon salt
- 1 cup white chocolate chips
- 1 cup dried cranberries

Instructions:

1. **Preheat Oven:** Preheat your oven to 350°F (175°C) and line a baking sheet with parchment paper.
2. **Cream Butter and Sugars:** In a large bowl, use an electric mixer to cream together the butter, granulated sugar, and brown sugar until light and fluffy.
3. **Add Eggs and Vanilla:** Beat in the eggs one at a time, followed by the vanilla extract, mixing until well combined.
4. **Combine Dry Ingredients:** In a separate bowl, whisk together the flour, baking soda, baking powder, and salt.
5. **Mix Dry and Wet Ingredients:** Gradually add the dry ingredients to the wet ingredients, mixing on low speed until just combined.
6. **Add Mix-ins:** Fold in the white chocolate chips and dried cranberries using a spatula or wooden spoon.
7. **Shape Cookies:** Scoop tablespoon-sized balls of dough onto the prepared baking sheet, spacing them about 2 inches apart.
8. **Bake:** Bake for 10-12 minutes, or until the edges are golden brown and the centers are set. The cookies will continue to cook slightly as they cool on the baking sheet.
9. **Cool:** Allow the cookies to cool on the baking sheet for 5 minutes before transferring them to a wire rack to cool completely.

Enjoy your delightful White Chocolate Cranberry Cookies with a cup of tea or coffee!

Chocolate Chia Pudding

Ingredients:

- 1/2 cup chia seeds
- 2 cups almond milk (or any plant-based milk)
- 1/4 cup unsweetened cocoa powder
- 1/4 cup pure maple syrup (or honey, if not vegan)
- 1 teaspoon vanilla extract
- A pinch of sea salt
- Optional toppings: fresh berries, sliced bananas, shredded coconut, or a dollop of almond butter

Instructions:

1. **Mix Ingredients:** In a medium bowl, whisk together the almond milk, cocoa powder, maple syrup, vanilla extract, and sea salt until well combined.
2. **Add Chia Seeds:** Stir in the chia seeds, making sure they are evenly distributed throughout the mixture.
3. **Refrigerate:** Cover the bowl with plastic wrap or a lid and refrigerate for at least 4 hours, or overnight. The chia seeds will absorb the liquid and expand, creating a pudding-like texture.
4. **Stir and Serve:** After the chia pudding has set, give it a good stir to break up any clumps and to ensure a smooth consistency.
5. **Add Toppings:** Divide the pudding into serving bowls and add your favorite toppings such as fresh berries, sliced bananas, shredded coconut, or a dollop of almond butter.

Enjoy your creamy, chocolatey, and nutritious chia pudding!

Raspberry Chocolate Ganache Tart

Ingredients:

For the Crust:

- 1 1/2 cups almond flour
- 1/4 cup cocoa powder
- 1/4 cup coconut oil (solid, not melted)
- 2 tablespoons maple syrup or honey
- 1/4 teaspoon sea salt

For the Ganache:

- 1 cup dark chocolate chips (or chopped dark chocolate)
- 1 cup full-fat coconut milk (or heavy cream if not vegan)
- 1 teaspoon vanilla extract
- 1 tablespoon maple syrup or honey (optional, for added sweetness)

For the Raspberry Layer:

- 1 cup fresh raspberries
- 2 tablespoons maple syrup or honey
- 1 teaspoon lemon juice

Instructions:

1. **Prepare the Crust:**
   - Preheat your oven to 350°F (175°C) and lightly grease a 9-inch tart pan.
   - In a medium bowl, mix together the almond flour, cocoa powder, coconut oil, maple syrup, and sea salt until the mixture resembles coarse crumbs.
   - Press the mixture evenly into the bottom and up the sides of the tart pan.
   - Bake for 10-12 minutes, until the crust is set. Let it cool completely.
2. **Prepare the Ganache:**
   - In a heatproof bowl, combine the dark chocolate chips and coconut milk.
   - Heat over a pot of simmering water (double boiler method) or in the microwave in 30-second intervals, stirring frequently, until the chocolate is completely melted and smooth.
   - Stir in the vanilla extract and maple syrup if using. Let the ganache cool slightly.
3. **Assemble the Tart:**
   - Pour the ganache into the cooled tart crust, spreading it evenly with a spatula.
   - Refrigerate for at least 2 hours, or until the ganache is set.
4. **Prepare the Raspberry Layer:**
   - In a small saucepan, combine the raspberries, maple syrup, and lemon juice.

- Cook over medium heat, gently mashing the raspberries with a spoon, until the mixture is slightly thickened (about 5 minutes).
- Let the raspberry mixture cool to room temperature.

5. **Finish the Tart:**
   - Once the ganache is set, spread the raspberry layer over the top.
   - Garnish with additional fresh raspberries or a sprinkle of sea salt if desired.
6. **Serve:**
   - Slice and serve chilled. Enjoy the rich combination of chocolate ganache and tangy raspberries!

This tart combines a rich chocolate ganache with a fresh raspberry topping for a truly indulgent dessert.

Chocolate Espresso Mousse

Ingredients:

- 1 cup heavy cream (or coconut cream for a dairy-free version)
- 1/2 cup dark chocolate chips or chopped dark chocolate
- 2 tablespoons espresso or strong coffee, cooled
- 2 tablespoons granulated sugar
- 1 teaspoon vanilla extract
- A pinch of salt

Instructions:

1. **Melt the Chocolate:**
   - In a heatproof bowl, melt the dark chocolate over a pot of simmering water (double boiler method) or in the microwave in 30-second intervals, stirring frequently. Once melted, let it cool slightly.
2. **Whip the Cream:**
   - In a medium bowl, whip the heavy cream with an electric mixer until soft peaks form.
   - Gradually add the granulated sugar while continuing to whip until stiff peaks form.
3. **Combine Ingredients:**
   - Gently fold the melted chocolate into the whipped cream until well combined and smooth.
   - Stir in the cooled espresso or strong coffee, vanilla extract, and a pinch of salt. Fold gently until fully incorporated.
4. **Chill:**
   - Spoon the mousse into serving dishes or glasses.
   - Refrigerate for at least 1 hour to allow the mousse to set and the flavors to meld.
5. **Serve:**
   - Garnish with chocolate shavings, a dollop of whipped cream, or a dusting of cocoa powder if desired.
   - Serve chilled and enjoy the rich, chocolatey, and coffee-infused dessert!

This Chocolate Espresso Mousse offers a delightful blend of creamy chocolate and bold espresso flavors, perfect for a sophisticated treat.

Chocolate Almond Cake

Ingredients:

For the Cake:

- 1 cup almond flour
- 1/2 cup cocoa powder
- 1 cup granulated sugar
- 1/2 teaspoon baking powder
- 1/4 teaspoon baking soda
- 1/4 teaspoon salt
- 4 large eggs
- 1/2 cup unsweetened applesauce (or vegetable oil)
- 1 teaspoon vanilla extract
- 1/2 cup milk (dairy or plant-based)

For the Chocolate Ganache (Optional):

- 1 cup dark chocolate chips (or chopped dark chocolate)
- 1/2 cup heavy cream (or full-fat coconut milk for a dairy-free version)
- 1 tablespoon maple syrup or honey (optional, for added sweetness)

For Garnish (Optional):

- Sliced almonds
- Fresh berries

Instructions:

1. **Preheat Oven:**
   - Preheat your oven to 350°F (175°C). Grease and flour an 8-inch round cake pan, or line it with parchment paper.
2. **Prepare the Cake Batter:**
   - In a large bowl, whisk together the almond flour, cocoa powder, granulated sugar, baking powder, baking soda, and salt.
   - In another bowl, beat the eggs until well combined. Stir in the applesauce (or oil), vanilla extract, and milk.
   - Gradually add the wet ingredients to the dry ingredients, mixing until just combined.
3. **Bake the Cake:**
   - Pour the batter into the prepared cake pan and smooth the top with a spatula.
   - Bake for 25-30 minutes, or until a toothpick inserted into the center comes out clean.

- Allow the cake to cool in the pan for 10 minutes before transferring it to a wire rack to cool completely.

4. **Prepare the Ganache (Optional):**
   - In a heatproof bowl, combine the dark chocolate chips and heavy cream.
   - Heat over a pot of simmering water (double boiler method) or in the microwave in 30-second intervals, stirring frequently, until the chocolate is completely melted and smooth.
   - Stir in the maple syrup or honey if desired, then let the ganache cool slightly before spreading over the cooled cake.

5. **Garnish and Serve:**
   - Once the ganache is set, garnish the cake with sliced almonds and fresh berries if desired.
   - Slice and serve. Enjoy the rich, chocolatey goodness with a hint of almond flavor!

This Chocolate Almond Cake is perfect for any occasion, combining the rich taste of chocolate with the nutty flavor of almonds for a truly indulgent dessert.

Chocolate Dipped Marshmallows

Ingredients:

- 1 bag of large marshmallows
- 1 cup dark chocolate chips (or semi-sweet chocolate chips)
- 1 tablespoon coconut oil or vegetable oil (to thin the chocolate)
- Sprinkles, crushed nuts, or shredded coconut (optional, for garnish)
- Parchment paper or a silicone baking mat (for cooling)

Instructions:

1. **Prepare Ingredients:**
   - Line a baking sheet with parchment paper or a silicone baking mat.
2. **Melt the Chocolate:**
   - In a heatproof bowl, combine the chocolate chips and coconut oil (or vegetable oil).
   - Melt the chocolate over a pot of simmering water (double boiler method) or in the microwave in 30-second intervals, stirring frequently until smooth and fully melted.
3. **Dip the Marshmallows:**
   - Holding each marshmallow by the stick (or skewer), dip it into the melted chocolate, covering about two-thirds of the marshmallow. Allow any excess chocolate to drip off.
   - If using, sprinkle the dipped marshmallows with your choice of toppings like sprinkles, crushed nuts, or shredded coconut while the chocolate is still wet.
4. **Cool and Set:**
   - Place the dipped marshmallows on the prepared baking sheet.
   - Allow the chocolate to set at room temperature. For faster setting, you can place the baking sheet in the refrigerator for about 15-20 minutes.
5. **Serve:**
   - Once the chocolate is fully set, remove the marshmallows from the baking sheet and serve.

These Chocolate Dipped Marshmallows are perfect for a sweet treat, party favors, or even a fun activity with kids. Enjoy your delightful combination of gooey marshmallows and rich chocolate!

Chocolate Mint Brownies

Ingredients:

For the Brownies:

- 1/2 cup (1 stick) unsalted butter
- 1 cup granulated sugar
- 2 large eggs
- 1 teaspoon vanilla extract
- 1/2 cup unsweetened cocoa powder
- 1/2 cup all-purpose flour
- 1/4 teaspoon salt
- 1/4 teaspoon baking powder
- 1/2 cup semi-sweet chocolate chips (optional, for extra gooey brownies)

For the Mint Frosting:

- 1/2 cup (1 stick) unsalted butter, softened
- 1 1/2 cups powdered sugar
- 2 tablespoons milk (dairy or plant-based)
- 1/2 teaspoon peppermint extract (adjust to taste)
- Green food coloring (optional)

For the Chocolate Ganache:

- 1/2 cup semi-sweet chocolate chips
- 1/4 cup heavy cream (or coconut cream for a dairy-free version)

Instructions:

1. **Preheat Oven:**
    - Preheat your oven to 350°F (175°C). Grease and flour an 8-inch square baking pan or line it with parchment paper.
2. **Make the Brownies:**
    - In a medium saucepan, melt the butter over low heat. Remove from heat and stir in the sugar, eggs, and vanilla extract until well combined.
    - Beat in the cocoa powder, flour, salt, and baking powder until smooth. If using chocolate chips, fold them into the batter.
    - Pour the batter into the prepared pan and spread evenly.
    - Bake for 20-25 minutes, or until a toothpick inserted into the center comes out with a few moist crumbs. Let the brownies cool completely in the pan on a wire rack.
3. **Prepare the Mint Frosting:**
    - In a medium bowl, beat the softened butter with an electric mixer until creamy.

- Gradually add the powdered sugar, mixing on low speed until combined.
- Add the milk, peppermint extract, and a few drops of green food coloring if using. Beat on high speed until the frosting is light and fluffy.

4. **Prepare the Chocolate Ganache:**
   - In a heatproof bowl, combine the chocolate chips and heavy cream.
   - Heat over a pot of simmering water (double boiler method) or in the microwave in 30-second intervals, stirring frequently until the chocolate is melted and smooth.
5. **Assemble the Brownies:**
   - Once the brownies have cooled, spread the mint frosting evenly over the top.
   - Drizzle the chocolate ganache over the frosting. Use a knife or spatula to swirl the ganache slightly for a marbled effect.
6. **Serve:**
   - Allow the ganache to set before cutting the brownies into squares. Enjoy!

These Chocolate Mint Brownies offer a delightful combination of rich chocolate and refreshing mint flavors, perfect for any dessert lover.

Caramel Chocolate Cheesecake

Ingredients:

For the Crust:

- 1 1/2 cups graham cracker crumbs (about 10-12 crackers)
- 1/4 cup granulated sugar
- 1/2 cup unsalted butter, melted

For the Cheesecake Filling:

- 4 (8-ounce) packages cream cheese, softened
- 1 cup granulated sugar
- 4 large eggs
- 1 cup sour cream
- 1 teaspoon vanilla extract
- 1/2 cup heavy cream
- 1/2 cup semi-sweet chocolate chips

For the Caramel Sauce:

- 1 cup granulated sugar
- 6 tablespoons unsalted butter, cut into pieces
- 1/2 cup heavy cream
- 1/4 teaspoon sea salt (optional)

For Garnish:

- Additional caramel sauce
- Whipped cream
- Chocolate shavings or chips

Instructions:

1. **Prepare the Crust:**
   - Preheat your oven to 350°F (175°C). Grease the bottom and sides of a 9-inch springform pan or line it with parchment paper.
   - In a medium bowl, mix the graham cracker crumbs, granulated sugar, and melted butter until the mixture resembles wet sand.
   - Press the mixture firmly into the bottom of the prepared pan to form an even crust.
   - Bake for 8-10 minutes, then let it cool while you prepare the filling.
2. **Prepare the Cheesecake Filling:**

- In a large bowl, beat the cream cheese with an electric mixer until smooth and creamy.
- Gradually add the sugar and beat until fully incorporated.
- Add the eggs one at a time, mixing well after each addition.
- Mix in the sour cream and vanilla extract until smooth.
- In a small saucepan, heat the heavy cream over medium heat until just simmering. Remove from heat and stir in the chocolate chips until melted and smooth. Let it cool slightly.
- Gently fold the chocolate mixture into the cheesecake filling until well combined.
- Pour the filling over the cooled crust and smooth the top.

3. **Bake the Cheesecake:**
   - Bake in the preheated oven for 55-65 minutes, or until the edges are set and the center is slightly jiggly.
   - Turn off the oven and leave the cheesecake in the oven with the door slightly ajar for 1 hour to cool gradually. This helps prevent cracks.
   - Remove from the oven and refrigerate for at least 4 hours, or overnight.

4. **Prepare the Caramel Sauce:**
   - In a medium saucepan over medium heat, melt the sugar until it turns a deep amber color, swirling the pan occasionally to ensure even melting.
   - Once the sugar is melted, carefully add the butter and stir until fully combined. The mixture will bubble vigorously.
   - Slowly pour in the heavy cream while stirring constantly. Continue to cook until smooth and slightly thickened.
   - Remove from heat and stir in the sea salt, if using. Let it cool to room temperature.

5. **Assemble the Cheesecake:**
   - Once the cheesecake is fully chilled, remove it from the springform pan.
   - Drizzle the cooled caramel sauce over the top of the cheesecake.
   - Garnish with whipped cream and chocolate shavings or chips if desired.

6. **Serve:**
   - Slice and serve chilled. Enjoy the rich layers of chocolate and caramel in every bite!

This Caramel Chocolate Cheesecake is a show-stopping dessert that combines creamy cheesecake with luscious caramel and chocolate flavors. Perfect for special occasions or any time you want to treat yourself!

Chocolate Coconut Smoothie

Ingredients:

- 1 cup coconut milk (or any plant-based milk)
- 1/2 cup Greek yogurt (or dairy-free yogurt for a vegan option)
- 1 banana, frozen
- 2 tablespoons unsweetened cocoa powder
- 2 tablespoons shredded coconut
- 1-2 tablespoons honey or maple syrup (to taste)
- 1/2 teaspoon vanilla extract
- A pinch of sea salt
- Ice cubes (optional, for a thicker smoothie)

Instructions:

1. **Blend Ingredients:**
   - In a blender, combine the coconut milk, Greek yogurt, frozen banana, cocoa powder, shredded coconut, honey (or maple syrup), vanilla extract, and a pinch of sea salt.
   - Blend until smooth and creamy. If the smoothie is too thick, you can add a bit more coconut milk or water to reach your desired consistency.
2. **Adjust Sweetness:**
   - Taste the smoothie and adjust the sweetness by adding more honey or maple syrup if needed. Blend again to combine.
3. **Serve:**
   - Pour the smoothie into glasses. If desired, add a few ice cubes and blend again for a colder and thicker texture.
4. **Garnish (Optional):**
   - Garnish with additional shredded coconut, chocolate shavings, or a slice of banana for a decorative touch.

Enjoy your creamy, chocolatey, and tropical smoothie!

Dark Chocolate Cherry Bark

Ingredients:

- 12 ounces dark chocolate (60% or higher cocoa content), chopped
- 1 cup dried cherries
- 1/2 cup chopped nuts (such as almonds or pistachios, optional)
- Sea salt flakes (optional, for garnish)

Instructions:

1. **Prepare a Baking Sheet:**
    - Line a baking sheet with parchment paper or a silicone baking mat. This will make it easier to remove the bark once it's set.
2. **Melt the Chocolate:**
    - In a heatproof bowl, melt the dark chocolate over a pot of simmering water (double boiler method) or in the microwave in 30-second intervals, stirring frequently until smooth and fully melted.
3. **Assemble the Bark:**
    - Pour the melted chocolate onto the prepared baking sheet and spread it into an even layer using a spatula.
    - While the chocolate is still melted, sprinkle the dried cherries evenly over the top.
    - If using, sprinkle the chopped nuts over the cherries. You can gently press them into the chocolate to ensure they stick.
4. **Garnish:**
    - Optionally, sprinkle a few sea salt flakes over the top for a touch of flavor contrast.
5. **Cool and Set:**
    - Refrigerate the bark for at least 1 hour, or until the chocolate is completely set and firm.
6. **Break into Pieces:**
    - Once the bark is set, break it into pieces or shards.
7. **Serve or Store:**
    - Enjoy immediately or store in an airtight container in a cool place for up to 2 weeks.

This Dark Chocolate Cherry Bark combines the rich flavors of dark chocolate with the tartness of dried cherries and optional crunch from nuts, making it a delightful and easy-to-make treat.

Hazelnut Chocolate Cake

Ingredients:

For the Cake:

- 1 cup (8 oz) unsalted butter, softened
- 1 cup granulated sugar
- 1/2 cup packed brown sugar
- 4 large eggs
- 1 teaspoon vanilla extract
- 1 cup all-purpose flour
- 1 cup hazelnut flour (finely ground)
- 1/2 cup unsweetened cocoa powder
- 1 teaspoon baking powder
- 1/2 teaspoon baking soda
- 1/4 teaspoon salt
- 1/2 cup whole milk

For the Chocolate Ganache:

- 1 cup semi-sweet chocolate chips or chopped chocolate
- 1/2 cup heavy cream

For the Hazelnut Crunch (Optional):

- 1/2 cup chopped hazelnuts
- 1/4 cup granulated sugar

Instructions:

1. **Prepare the Cake Batter:**
    - Preheat your oven to 350°F (175°C). Grease and flour a 9-inch round cake pan or line it with parchment paper.
    - In a large bowl, cream together the softened butter, granulated sugar, and brown sugar until light and fluffy.
    - Beat in the eggs one at a time, mixing well after each addition. Stir in the vanilla extract.
    - In another bowl, whisk together the flour, hazelnut flour, cocoa powder, baking powder, baking soda, and salt.
    - Gradually add the dry ingredients to the wet ingredients, alternating with the milk, beginning and ending with the dry ingredients. Mix until just combined.
2. **Bake the Cake:**
    - Pour the batter into the prepared cake pan and smooth the top with a spatula.

- Bake for 25-30 minutes, or until a toothpick inserted into the center comes out clean.
- Allow the cake to cool in the pan for 10 minutes before transferring it to a wire rack to cool completely.

3. **Prepare the Ganache:**
   - In a heatproof bowl, combine the chocolate chips and heavy cream.
   - Heat over a pot of simmering water (double boiler method) or in the microwave in 30-second intervals, stirring frequently until smooth and fully melted. Let it cool slightly.

4. **Prepare the Hazelnut Crunch (Optional):**
   - In a small skillet, toast the chopped hazelnuts over medium heat until golden brown and fragrant.
   - Remove from heat and sprinkle with granulated sugar. Stir until the sugar has melted and coated the hazelnuts. Let cool.

5. **Assemble the Cake:**
   - Once the cake is completely cool, spread the chocolate ganache evenly over the top and sides of the cake.
   - If using, sprinkle the hazelnut crunch over the top of the ganache while it is still soft, or gently press it into the sides.

6. **Serve:**
   - Slice and serve. Enjoy your indulgent Hazelnut Chocolate Cake!

This Hazelnut Chocolate Cake combines the nutty flavor of hazelnuts with rich chocolate for a deliciously moist and satisfying dessert. Perfect for special occasions or a delightful treat!

Chocolate Covered Caramel Apples

Ingredients:

For the Caramel:

- 1 cup granulated sugar
- 6 tablespoons unsalted butter, cut into pieces
- 1/2 cup heavy cream
- 1/4 teaspoon sea salt (optional)

For the Apples:

- 4 medium apples (Granny Smith or Honeycrisp work well)
- 4 wooden sticks or skewers
- 1 cup semi-sweet chocolate chips (or chopped dark chocolate)
- 1 tablespoon coconut oil or vegetable oil (to thin the chocolate)
- Toppings (optional): chopped nuts, sprinkles, crushed candy, or sea salt

Instructions:

1. **Prepare the Apples:**
   - Wash and thoroughly dry the apples. Remove the stems and insert the sticks into the top of each apple, pushing about halfway through.
   - Place the apples on a baking sheet lined with parchment paper or a silicone baking mat.
2. **Make the Caramel:**
   - In a medium saucepan, heat the granulated sugar over medium heat, stirring constantly with a heat-resistant spatula or wooden spoon. The sugar will clump and then melt into a smooth, amber-colored liquid.
   - Once the sugar is fully melted and golden brown, carefully add the butter and stir until fully combined. The mixture will bubble vigorously.
   - Slowly pour in the heavy cream while stirring constantly. Continue to cook and stir until the caramel is smooth and thickened.
   - Remove from heat and stir in sea salt if using.
3. **Dip the Apples in Caramel:**
   - Working quickly, dip each apple into the caramel, swirling it to coat the apple evenly. Let the excess caramel drip off.
   - Place the caramel-coated apples back on the prepared baking sheet. Allow the caramel to set and harden at room temperature or in the refrigerator.
4. **Prepare the Chocolate:**
   - In a heatproof bowl, combine the chocolate chips and coconut oil (or vegetable oil).

- Melt the chocolate over a pot of simmering water (double boiler method) or in the microwave in 30-second intervals, stirring frequently until smooth and fully melted.
5. **Dip the Apples in Chocolate:**
    - Once the caramel has set, dip each apple into the melted chocolate, swirling to coat. Allow the excess chocolate to drip off.
    - Return the chocolate-coated apples to the baking sheet.
6. **Add Toppings (Optional):**
    - Before the chocolate sets, sprinkle the apples with your choice of toppings, such as chopped nuts, sprinkles, crushed candy, or a pinch of sea salt.
7. **Cool and Set:**
    - Allow the chocolate to set at room temperature or in the refrigerator.
8. **Serve:**
    - Once the chocolate has hardened, the apples are ready to serve. Enjoy your delicious and festive Chocolate Covered Caramel Apples!

These Chocolate Covered Caramel Apples are a delightful treat combining the richness of caramel, the smoothness of chocolate, and optional toppings for added crunch and flavor. Perfect for fall festivities or as a sweet gift!

Strawberry Chocolate Shortcake

Ingredients:

For the Shortcake Biscuits:

- 2 cups all-purpose flour
- 1/4 cup granulated sugar
- 1 tablespoon baking powder
- 1/2 teaspoon salt
- 1/2 cup unsalted butter, cold and cut into small cubes
- 2/3 cup whole milk (or plant-based milk)

For the Chocolate Ganache:

- 1 cup semi-sweet chocolate chips (or chopped dark chocolate)
- 1/2 cup heavy cream (or full-fat coconut milk for a dairy-free option)

For the Strawberries:

- 4 cups fresh strawberries, hulled and sliced
- 1/4 cup granulated sugar
- 1 teaspoon lemon juice

For Whipped Cream:

- 1 cup heavy cream (or coconut cream for a dairy-free option)
- 2 tablespoons powdered sugar
- 1 teaspoon vanilla extract

Instructions:

1. **Prepare the Strawberries:**
    - In a bowl, combine the sliced strawberries, granulated sugar, and lemon juice. Toss to coat and let sit for at least 30 minutes to allow the strawberries to release their juices and become slightly syrupy.
2. **Make the Shortcake Biscuits:**
    - Preheat your oven to 425°F (220°C). Line a baking sheet with parchment paper.
    - In a large bowl, whisk together the flour, granulated sugar, baking powder, and salt.
    - Cut in the cold butter using a pastry cutter or your fingers until the mixture resembles coarse crumbs.
    - Gradually add the milk, stirring until just combined. Do not overmix.

- Turn the dough out onto a floured surface and gently knead it a few times. Pat or roll the dough to about 1-inch thickness. Cut into rounds using a biscuit cutter or glass.
- Place the biscuits on the prepared baking sheet and bake for 12-15 minutes, or until golden brown. Let cool slightly.

3. **Prepare the Chocolate Ganache:**
   - In a heatproof bowl, combine the chocolate chips and heavy cream.
   - Melt the chocolate over a pot of simmering water (double boiler method) or in the microwave in 30-second intervals, stirring frequently until smooth and glossy. Let cool slightly.

4. **Make the Whipped Cream:**
   - In a chilled bowl, beat the heavy cream with an electric mixer until soft peaks form.
   - Add the powdered sugar and vanilla extract, and continue to beat until stiff peaks form.

5. **Assemble the Strawberry Chocolate Shortcake:**
   - Slice the shortcake biscuits in half horizontally.
   - Drizzle or spread a layer of chocolate ganache on the bottom half of each biscuit.
   - Spoon some of the macerated strawberries over the ganache.
   - Top with a generous dollop of whipped cream.
   - Place the top half of the biscuit over the whipped cream.

6. **Serve:**
   - Garnish with additional chocolate ganache, strawberries, or a sprinkle of powdered sugar if desired.
   - Serve immediately and enjoy!

This Strawberry Chocolate Shortcake combines the rich flavors of chocolate with fresh, sweet strawberries and fluffy shortcake biscuits, making it a perfect dessert for any occasion.

Chocolate Banana Bread

Ingredients:

- 1/2 cup (1 stick) unsalted butter, softened
- 1 cup granulated sugar
- 2 large eggs
- 1 teaspoon vanilla extract
- 3 ripe bananas, mashed (about 1 1/2 cups)
- 1 1/2 cups all-purpose flour
- 1/2 cup unsweetened cocoa powder
- 1 teaspoon baking powder
- 1/2 teaspoon baking soda
- 1/4 teaspoon salt
- 1/2 cup semi-sweet chocolate chips (optional, for added chocolatey goodness)

Instructions:

1. **Preheat Oven:**
    - Preheat your oven to 350°F (175°C). Grease and flour a 9x5-inch loaf pan, or line it with parchment paper.
2. **Prepare the Batter:**
    - In a large bowl, cream together the softened butter and granulated sugar until light and fluffy.
    - Beat in the eggs one at a time, then stir in the vanilla extract.
    - Mix in the mashed bananas until well combined.
    - In another bowl, whisk together the flour, cocoa powder, baking powder, baking soda, and salt.
    - Gradually add the dry ingredients to the wet ingredients, mixing until just combined. Be careful not to overmix.
    - If using, fold in the chocolate chips.
3. **Bake the Bread:**
    - Pour the batter into the prepared loaf pan and smooth the top with a spatula.
    - Bake for 60-70 minutes, or until a toothpick inserted into the center of the loaf comes out clean or with just a few moist crumbs.
    - If the top starts to get too dark before the center is cooked, you can tent the bread with aluminum foil.
4. **Cool:**
    - Allow the bread to cool in the pan for 10 minutes before transferring it to a wire rack to cool completely.
5. **Serve:**
    - Slice and serve. Enjoy the rich, chocolatey flavor with the natural sweetness of bananas.

This Chocolate Banana Bread is perfect for breakfast, a snack, or a dessert, offering a delightful combination of flavors and a moist, tender crumb.

Dark Chocolate Pudding

Ingredients:

- 2 3/4 cups whole milk (or plant-based milk for a dairy-free option)
- 1/2 cup granulated sugar
- 1/3 cup unsweetened dark cocoa powder
- 1/4 cup cornstarch
- 1/4 teaspoon salt
- 4 large egg yolks
- 2 tablespoons unsalted butter
- 1 teaspoon vanilla extract
- 1/2 cup dark chocolate chips or chopped dark chocolate (60% cocoa or higher)

Instructions:

1. **Combine Dry Ingredients:**
   - In a medium saucepan, whisk together the granulated sugar, cocoa powder, cornstarch, and salt.
2. **Add Milk:**
   - Gradually whisk in the milk until the mixture is smooth and free of lumps.
3. **Cook the Pudding:**
   - Place the saucepan over medium heat. Cook the mixture, whisking constantly, until it begins to simmer. Continue to cook for about 2-3 minutes, or until the mixture thickens and begins to bubble.
4. **Temper the Egg Yolks:**
   - In a separate bowl, lightly beat the egg yolks.
   - Gradually ladle about 1/2 cup of the hot chocolate mixture into the egg yolks while whisking constantly. This helps to temper the yolks and prevent them from curdling.
   - Slowly pour the tempered egg yolks back into the saucepan with the remaining chocolate mixture, whisking constantly.
5. **Finish Cooking:**
   - Continue to cook the pudding over medium heat, whisking constantly, for another 2-3 minutes until it is thick and creamy.
6. **Add Chocolate and Butter:**
   - Remove the saucepan from heat. Stir in the dark chocolate chips or chopped chocolate until melted and smooth.
   - Add the butter and vanilla extract, stirring until the butter is completely melted and incorporated.
7. **Cool and Serve:**
   - Pour the pudding into individual serving dishes or a large bowl. Cover with plastic wrap, pressing the wrap directly onto the surface of the pudding to prevent a skin from forming.

- Refrigerate for at least 2 hours, or until chilled and set.
8. **Garnish (Optional):**
    - Before serving, you can garnish with whipped cream, chocolate shavings, or fresh berries if desired.

Enjoy your silky, rich Dark Chocolate Pudding—perfect for satisfying your chocolate cravings with a touch of elegance!

Chocolate Bourbon Balls

Ingredients:

- 1 cup finely crushed graham crackers (about 8-10 whole crackers)
- 1 cup finely chopped nuts (such as walnuts or pecans)
- 1 cup powdered sugar
- 1/4 cup unsweetened cocoa powder
- 1/2 cup bourbon
- 1/2 cup dark chocolate chips or chopped dark chocolate
- 1 tablespoon unsalted butter
- Extra powdered sugar or cocoa powder (for rolling, optional)

Instructions:

1. **Prepare the Mixture:**
   - In a large bowl, combine the crushed graham crackers, chopped nuts, powdered sugar, and cocoa powder. Mix well to combine.
2. **Add Bourbon:**
   - Gradually stir in the bourbon until the mixture starts to come together. The mixture should be moist but not overly wet. If it's too dry, add a bit more bourbon; if too wet, add a bit more crushed graham crackers.
3. **Chill the Mixture:**
   - Cover the bowl and refrigerate the mixture for about 30 minutes to make it easier to handle.
4. **Form the Balls:**
   - Once chilled, scoop out small amounts of the mixture and roll them between your palms to form 1-inch balls. Place the balls on a baking sheet lined with parchment paper.
5. **Prepare the Chocolate Coating:**
   - In a heatproof bowl, combine the dark chocolate chips and butter.
   - Melt over a pot of simmering water (double boiler method) or in the microwave in 30-second intervals, stirring frequently until smooth and fully melted.
6. **Dip the Balls:**
   - Dip each ball into the melted chocolate, using a fork or toothpick to hold it. Allow any excess chocolate to drip off before placing the ball back on the parchment-lined baking sheet.
7. **Coat with Powdered Sugar or Cocoa Powder (Optional):**
   - While the chocolate is still wet, you can roll the balls in additional powdered sugar or cocoa powder for a finishing touch.
8. **Set the Chocolate:**
   - Refrigerate the chocolate-covered balls for at least 30 minutes, or until the chocolate is fully set.
9. **Serve:**

- - Once the chocolate has hardened, the Chocolate Bourbon Balls are ready to be enjoyed.

These Chocolate Bourbon Balls are perfect for holiday parties, special occasions, or as a treat to indulge in. Their rich chocolate flavor and subtle bourbon kick make them a sophisticated and delightful confection.

Chocolate Almond Milkshake

Ingredients:

- 1 cup almond milk (or any plant-based milk)
- 1/2 cup vanilla or chocolate almond milk ice cream (or dairy-free ice cream)
- 1/4 cup unsweetened cocoa powder
- 2 tablespoons almond butter
- 2 tablespoons honey or maple syrup (to taste)
- 1/4 teaspoon vanilla extract
- 1/2 cup ice cubes (optional, for a thicker milkshake)
- Whipped cream (optional, for garnish)
- Sliced almonds or chocolate shavings (optional, for garnish)

Instructions:

1. **Blend the Ingredients:**
   - In a blender, combine the almond milk, almond milk ice cream, cocoa powder, almond butter, honey (or maple syrup), and vanilla extract.
   - Blend until smooth and creamy. If you prefer a thicker milkshake, add the ice cubes and blend again until well combined.
2. **Taste and Adjust Sweetness:**
   - Taste the milkshake and adjust the sweetness if needed by adding more honey or maple syrup. Blend again if you make any adjustments.
3. **Serve:**
   - Pour the milkshake into a tall glass.
4. **Garnish (Optional):**
   - Top with whipped cream if desired.
   - Sprinkle sliced almonds or chocolate shavings over the whipped cream for added texture and flavor.
5. **Enjoy:**
   - Serve immediately with a straw and enjoy your indulgent Chocolate Almond Milkshake!

This milkshake combines the richness of chocolate with the nutty flavor of almonds, creating a creamy and satisfying treat that's perfect for any time of day.

Chocolate Peanut Butter Truffles

Ingredients:

For the Truffles:

- 1 cup creamy peanut butter (not natural, for smooth texture)
- 1 cup powdered sugar
- 1 cup crushed graham crackers (about 8-10 whole crackers)
- 1/2 cup semi-sweet chocolate chips or chopped dark chocolate
- 1/4 cup heavy cream

For Coating (Optional):

- 1 cup semi-sweet chocolate chips or chopped dark chocolate
- 1 tablespoon coconut oil or vegetable oil
- Chopped peanuts, cocoa powder, or sprinkles (for garnish, optional)

Instructions:

1. **Prepare the Peanut Butter Mixture:**
   - In a medium bowl, combine the creamy peanut butter, powdered sugar, and crushed graham crackers. Mix until fully combined and the mixture holds together when pressed.
2. **Form the Truffles:**
   - Roll the peanut butter mixture into small balls, about 1-inch in diameter. Place them on a baking sheet lined with parchment paper.
3. **Chill the Truffles:**
   - Refrigerate the truffles for about 30 minutes to firm them up, making them easier to dip in chocolate.
4. **Prepare the Chocolate Coating:**
   - In a heatproof bowl, combine the chocolate chips and heavy cream.
   - Melt over a pot of simmering water (double boiler method) or in the microwave in 30-second intervals, stirring frequently until smooth and glossy. If using the microwave, be careful not to overheat the chocolate.
5. **Dip the Truffles:**
   - Using a fork or toothpick, dip each chilled peanut butter ball into the melted chocolate, coating it completely. Allow any excess chocolate to drip off.
   - Return the coated truffles to the parchment-lined baking sheet.
6. **Garnish (Optional):**
   - Before the chocolate sets, you can sprinkle the truffles with chopped peanuts, cocoa powder, or sprinkles for extra texture and flavor.
7. **Cool and Set:**
   - Refrigerate the truffles for at least 30 minutes, or until the chocolate coating is set.

8. **Serve:**
    - Once set, the Chocolate Peanut Butter Truffles are ready to be enjoyed. Store any leftovers in an airtight container in the refrigerator for up to 2 weeks.

These truffles are a perfect combination of rich chocolate and creamy peanut butter, making them a delightful treat for any occasion.

Chocolate Orange Bundt Cake

Ingredients:

For the Cake:

- 1 3/4 cups all-purpose flour
- 1/2 cup unsweetened cocoa powder
- 1 1/2 teaspoons baking powder
- 1/2 teaspoon baking soda
- 1/4 teaspoon salt
- 1/2 cup unsalted butter, softened
- 1 cup granulated sugar
- 1/2 cup packed brown sugar
- 3 large eggs
- 1 teaspoon vanilla extract
- 1 cup orange juice (freshly squeezed for best flavor)
- 1 tablespoon finely grated orange zest
- 1/2 cup sour cream (or Greek yogurt for a lighter option)

For the Chocolate Glaze:

- 1/2 cup semi-sweet chocolate chips or chopped dark chocolate
- 1/4 cup heavy cream
- 1 tablespoon unsalted butter

For Garnish (Optional):

- Additional grated orange zest
- Fresh orange slices

Instructions:

1. **Preheat Oven:**
    - Preheat your oven to 350°F (175°C). Grease and flour a 10-cup Bundt pan or spray it with non-stick baking spray.
2. **Prepare the Cake Batter:**
    - In a medium bowl, whisk together the flour, cocoa powder, baking powder, baking soda, and salt.
    - In a large bowl, cream together the softened butter, granulated sugar, and brown sugar until light and fluffy.
    - Beat in the eggs one at a time, mixing well after each addition. Stir in the vanilla extract.
    - Add the orange juice and grated orange zest, mixing until combined.

- Gradually add the dry ingredients to the wet ingredients, alternating with the sour cream, beginning and ending with the dry ingredients. Mix until just combined.
3. **Bake the Cake:**
    - Pour the batter into the prepared Bundt pan and smooth the top with a spatula.
    - Bake for 50-60 minutes, or until a toothpick inserted into the center of the cake comes out clean.
    - Allow the cake to cool in the pan for 15 minutes before transferring it to a wire rack to cool completely.
4. **Prepare the Chocolate Glaze:**
    - In a heatproof bowl, combine the chocolate chips and heavy cream.
    - Melt over a pot of simmering water (double boiler method) or in the microwave in 30-second intervals, stirring frequently until smooth and glossy.
    - Stir in the butter until fully incorporated and the glaze is smooth.
5. **Glaze the Cake:**
    - Once the cake has cooled completely, drizzle the chocolate glaze over the top, allowing it to cascade down the sides.
6. **Garnish (Optional):**
    - Garnish with additional grated orange zest or fresh orange slices if desired.
7. **Serve:**
    - Slice and serve your Chocolate Orange Bundt Cake. Enjoy the delightful combination of chocolate and citrus!

This Chocolate Orange Bundt Cake is perfect for any occasion, offering a wonderful blend of rich chocolate and refreshing orange flavors in every bite.

Raspberry Chocolate Trifle

Ingredients:

For the Chocolate Cake:

- 1 cup all-purpose flour
- 1/2 cup unsweetened cocoa powder
- 1 cup granulated sugar
- 1 1/2 teaspoons baking powder
- 1/2 teaspoon baking soda
- 1/4 teaspoon salt
- 1/2 cup unsalted butter, softened
- 1/2 cup whole milk
- 2 large eggs
- 1 teaspoon vanilla extract
- 1/2 cup boiling water

For the Raspberry Filling:

- 2 cups fresh raspberries (or frozen, thawed)
- 1/4 cup granulated sugar
- 1 tablespoon lemon juice

For the Chocolate Ganache:

- 1 cup semi-sweet chocolate chips or chopped dark chocolate
- 1/2 cup heavy cream

For the Whipped Cream:

- 1 cup heavy cream
- 2 tablespoons powdered sugar
- 1 teaspoon vanilla extract

Instructions:

1. **Prepare the Chocolate Cake:**
    - Preheat your oven to 350°F (175°C). Grease and flour an 8-inch square baking pan or line it with parchment paper.
    - In a medium bowl, whisk together the flour, cocoa powder, sugar, baking powder, baking soda, and salt.
    - In a large bowl, cream the butter until light and fluffy. Beat in the eggs one at a time, then add the vanilla extract.

        - Gradually add the dry ingredients to the butter mixture, alternating with the milk, until just combined.
        - Stir in the boiling water until smooth (the batter will be thin).
        - Pour the batter into the prepared pan and bake for 25-30 minutes, or until a toothpick inserted into the center comes out clean.
        - Allow the cake to cool completely before cutting it into cubes.
2. **Prepare the Raspberry Filling:**
        - In a small saucepan, combine the raspberries, granulated sugar, and lemon juice.
        - Cook over medium heat, stirring occasionally, until the raspberries break down and the mixture thickens slightly, about 5-7 minutes.
        - Remove from heat and let cool.
3. **Prepare the Chocolate Ganache:**
        - In a heatproof bowl, combine the chocolate chips and heavy cream.
        - Melt over a pot of simmering water (double boiler method) or in the microwave in 30-second intervals, stirring frequently until smooth. Let cool slightly.
4. **Prepare the Whipped Cream:**
        - In a chilled bowl, beat the heavy cream, powdered sugar, and vanilla extract until soft peaks form.
5. **Assemble the Trifle:**
        - In a trifle dish or individual serving glasses, start by layering cubes of chocolate cake at the bottom.
        - Spoon a layer of raspberry filling over the cake.
        - Drizzle a layer of chocolate ganache over the raspberries.
        - Add a layer of whipped cream on top.
        - Repeat the layers as desired, ending with whipped cream on top.
6. **Chill and Serve:**
        - Refrigerate the trifle for at least 2 hours to allow the flavors to meld and the layers to set.
        - Before serving, you can garnish with fresh raspberries, chocolate shavings, or a mint leaf if desired.

Enjoy your elegant and indulgent Raspberry Chocolate Trifle, perfect for special occasions or as a luxurious treat!

Chocolate-Covered Rice Crispy Treats

Ingredients:

For the Rice Crispy Treats:

- 4 cups Rice Krispies cereal
- 3 tablespoons unsalted butter
- 1 package (10 oz) mini marshmallows (or 5 cups regular marshmallows)
- 1/2 teaspoon vanilla extract (optional)

For the Chocolate Coating:

- 1 cup semi-sweet chocolate chips or chopped dark chocolate
- 1/2 cup milk chocolate chips (optional for a blend of chocolate)
- 1 tablespoon coconut oil or vegetable oil (to help with smooth coating)

Instructions:

1. **Prepare the Rice Crispy Treats:**
   - **Grease a Pan:** Lightly grease a 9x13-inch baking pan or line it with parchment paper.
   - **Melt Butter:** In a large saucepan, melt the butter over low heat.
   - **Add Marshmallows:** Add the marshmallows to the melted butter and stir until completely melted and smooth. If using regular marshmallows, stir frequently until they are fully melted.
   - **Mix in Vanilla:** If desired, stir in the vanilla extract.
   - **Add Cereal:** Remove from heat and quickly add the Rice Krispies cereal, stirring until the cereal is well coated with the marshmallow mixture.
   - **Press into Pan:** Transfer the mixture to the prepared pan and press it down evenly with a spatula or the back of a spoon. Allow to cool completely and set.
2. **Prepare the Chocolate Coating:**
   - **Melt Chocolate:** In a heatproof bowl, combine the semi-sweet and milk chocolate chips (if using both) with the coconut oil.
   - **Heat:** Melt over a pot of simmering water (double boiler method) or in the microwave in 30-second intervals, stirring frequently until smooth and fully melted.
3. **Dip or Drizzle:**
   - **Cut the Treats:** Once the Rice Crispy Treats have cooled and set, cut them into squares or bars.
   - **Coat with Chocolate:**
     - **Dipping Method:** Dip each Rice Crispy treat into the melted chocolate, covering it about halfway. Place the coated treats back on the parchment-lined baking sheet.
     - **Drizzling Method:** If you prefer a lighter coating, you can use a spoon to drizzle the melted chocolate over the treats.
4. **Set the Chocolate:**

- **Cool:** Allow the chocolate coating to set at room temperature. You can speed up the process by placing the treats in the refrigerator for about 15-20 minutes.
5. **Serve:**
    - **Enjoy:** Once the chocolate has hardened, the Chocolate-Covered Rice Crispy Treats are ready to be enjoyed.

Tips:

- **Add Toppings:** For extra flair, you can sprinkle the chocolate-covered treats with sprinkles, crushed nuts, or sea salt before the chocolate sets.
- **Storage:** Store the treats in an airtight container at room temperature or in the refrigerator for up to a week.

These Chocolate-Covered Rice Crispy Treats offer a delightful combination of crispy, chewy, and chocolatey goodness, perfect for snacks, parties, or a sweet indulgence!

S'mores Chocolate Bars

Ingredients:

For the Graham Cracker Base:

- 1 1/2 cups graham cracker crumbs (about 10-12 graham crackers, crushed)
- 1/4 cup granulated sugar
- 1/2 cup unsalted butter, melted

For the Chocolate Layer:

- 1 cup semi-sweet chocolate chips or chopped dark chocolate
- 1 cup milk chocolate chips or chopped milk chocolate
- 1/2 cup heavy cream

For the Marshmallow Layer:

- 2 cups mini marshmallows (or 1 1/2 cups regular marshmallows, cut into smaller pieces)

Instructions:

1. **Prepare the Graham Cracker Base:**
   - **Preheat Oven:** Preheat your oven to 350°F (175°C). Line an 8x8-inch baking pan with parchment paper or foil, leaving an overhang for easy removal.
   - **Mix Crumbs:** In a medium bowl, combine graham cracker crumbs, granulated sugar, and melted butter. Mix until the crumbs are evenly coated with butter and the mixture resembles wet sand.
   - **Press Into Pan:** Press the graham cracker mixture firmly into the bottom of the prepared pan to create an even base.
   - **Bake:** Bake for 8-10 minutes, or until the crust is lightly golden. Remove from the oven and let it cool slightly.
2. **Prepare the Chocolate Layer:**
   - **Heat Cream:** In a small saucepan, heat the heavy cream over medium heat until it just begins to simmer.
   - **Melt Chocolate:** In a heatproof bowl, combine the semi-sweet and milk chocolate chips. Pour the hot cream over the chocolate and let it sit for 1-2 minutes.
   - **Stir Until Smooth:** Stir the mixture until the chocolate is completely melted and smooth.
   - **Spread Chocolate:** Pour the chocolate mixture over the graham cracker crust and spread it evenly with a spatula.
3. **Add the Marshmallows:**
   - **Top with Marshmallows:** Evenly sprinkle the mini marshmallows over the chocolate layer.
4. **Broil to Toast:**
   - **Toast Marshmallows:** Place the pan under the broiler for 1-2 minutes, or until the marshmallows are golden brown and toasted. Watch closely to prevent burning.

- **Cool:** Allow the bars to cool completely in the pan on a wire rack.
5. **Cut and Serve:**
    - **Remove from Pan:** Once cool, lift the bars out of the pan using the parchment paper or foil overhang.
    - **Cut into Squares:** Cut into squares or rectangles with a sharp knife.
    - **Enjoy:** Serve and enjoy your S'mores Chocolate Bars!

Tips:

- **Storage:** Store leftover bars in an airtight container at room temperature for up to a week, or in the refrigerator for longer freshness.
- **For Extra Crunch:** Add a sprinkle of sea salt on top of the marshmallows before broiling for a sweet and salty contrast.

These S'mores Chocolate Bars bring the nostalgic taste of campfire s'mores into a convenient, easy-to-make treat that everyone will love!

Spicy Chocolate Chili

Ingredients:

For the Chili:

- 2 tablespoons olive oil
- 1 large onion, diced
- 4 cloves garlic, minced
- 1 bell pepper, diced (any color)
- 1 carrot, diced
- 1 celery stalk, diced
- 1 pound ground beef (or ground turkey or a plant-based alternative)
- 2 tablespoons chili powder
- 1 tablespoon smoked paprika
- 1 teaspoon ground cumin
- 1/2 teaspoon cayenne pepper (adjust to taste)
- 1/2 teaspoon ground cinnamon
- 1 can (14.5 oz) diced tomatoes
- 1 can (15 oz) kidney beans, drained and rinsed
- 1 can (15 oz) black beans, drained and rinsed
- 1 cup beef or vegetable broth
- 2 tablespoons tomato paste
- 2 tablespoons dark chocolate (70% cocoa or higher), chopped or chips
- Salt and black pepper to taste

For Garnish (Optional):

- Shredded cheese
- Sour cream or Greek yogurt
- Chopped fresh cilantro
- Sliced jalapeños
- Crumbled tortilla chips

Instructions:

1. **Sauté Vegetables:**
   - Heat the olive oil in a large pot or Dutch oven over medium heat.
   - Add the diced onion and cook until softened, about 5 minutes.
   - Add the garlic, bell pepper, carrot, and celery. Cook for an additional 5-7 minutes until the vegetables start to soften.
2. **Cook the Meat:**
   - Add the ground beef (or your chosen protein) to the pot. Cook until browned, breaking it up with a spoon as it cooks. Drain any excess fat if needed.
3. **Add Spices:**
   - Stir in the chili powder, smoked paprika, cumin, cayenne pepper, and cinnamon. Cook for about 1 minute until fragrant.
4. **Add Remaining Ingredients:**

        - Add the diced tomatoes, kidney beans, black beans, beef or vegetable broth, and tomato paste. Stir to combine.
5. **Simmer the Chili:**
    - Bring the mixture to a boil. Reduce heat to low and let the chili simmer for 30-40 minutes, stirring occasionally, until the flavors meld and the chili thickens.
6. **Incorporate Chocolate:**
    - Stir in the chopped dark chocolate until melted and fully incorporated into the chili. Adjust seasoning with salt and black pepper to taste.
7. **Serve:**
    - Ladle the chili into bowls. Garnish with your choice of shredded cheese, sour cream, chopped cilantro, sliced jalapeños, or crumbled tortilla chips if desired.

Tips:

- **Adjust Heat:** Modify the amount of cayenne pepper to adjust the heat level to your preference. For a milder chili, reduce or omit the cayenne.
- **Make Ahead:** This chili can be made ahead of time and stored in the refrigerator for up to 4 days or frozen for up to 3 months. The flavors often improve after a day or two.
- **Chocolate Variations:** Experiment with different types of chocolate, such as milk or semi-sweet, depending on your sweetness preference.

Enjoy this Spicy Chocolate Chili for a comforting, savory meal with a surprising hint of rich chocolate flavor!

Chocolate Fig Bars

Ingredients:

For the Fig Filling:

- 1 cup dried figs, chopped (about 10-12 figs)
- 1/2 cup water
- 1/4 cup honey or maple syrup
- 1/2 teaspoon vanilla extract
- 1/2 teaspoon ground cinnamon (optional)

For the Chocolate Crust and Topping:

- 1 1/2 cups all-purpose flour
- 1/2 cup unsweetened cocoa powder
- 1/2 cup granulated sugar
- 1/4 teaspoon salt
- 1/2 cup unsalted butter, cold and cut into small pieces
- 1 large egg yolk
- 1/2 cup semi-sweet chocolate chips or chopped dark chocolate
- 2 tablespoons heavy cream

Instructions:

1. **Prepare the Fig Filling:**
    - **Simmer Figs:** In a small saucepan, combine the chopped figs, water, and honey (or maple syrup). Cook over medium heat, stirring occasionally, until the figs are softened and the mixture thickens, about 8-10 minutes.
    - **Blend Filling:** Transfer the mixture to a food processor or blender. Add the vanilla extract and cinnamon (if using) and blend until smooth. Set aside to cool.
2. **Prepare the Chocolate Crust:**
    - **Preheat Oven:** Preheat your oven to 350°F (175°C). Grease and line an 8x8-inch baking pan with parchment paper, leaving an overhang for easy removal.
    - **Mix Dry Ingredients:** In a medium bowl, whisk together the flour, cocoa powder, sugar, and salt.
    - **Cut in Butter:** Add the cold butter pieces to the dry ingredients. Use a pastry cutter or your fingers to work the butter into the flour mixture until it resembles coarse crumbs.
    - **Add Egg Yolk:** Stir in the egg yolk until the mixture starts to come together. Press about two-thirds of the mixture evenly into the bottom of the prepared pan to form the crust.
3. **Bake the Crust:**
    - **Bake Base:** Bake the crust for 12-15 minutes, or until set and slightly firm. Remove from the oven and let it cool slightly.
4. **Assemble the Bars:**

              - **Spread Filling:** Evenly spread the fig filling over the partially baked crust.
              - **Add Topping:** Crumble the remaining chocolate crust mixture over the fig filling.
5. **Bake the Bars:**
              - **Bake:** Return to the oven and bake for an additional 20-25 minutes, or until the topping is set and slightly crisp.
6. **Prepare the Chocolate Drizzle (Optional):**
              - **Melt Chocolate:** While the bars are baking, melt the chocolate chips and heavy cream together in a heatproof bowl over a pot of simmering water (double boiler method) or in the microwave in 30-second intervals, stirring until smooth.
              - **Drizzle:** Once the bars are cool, drizzle the melted chocolate over the top for an extra layer of decadence.
7. **Cool and Serve:**
              - **Cool Completely:** Allow the bars to cool completely in the pan on a wire rack. Lift out using the parchment paper overhang and cut into squares or bars.
              - **Enjoy:** Serve and enjoy your delicious Chocolate Fig Bars!

Tips:

- **Storage:** Store the bars in an airtight container at room temperature for up to a week, or in the refrigerator for up to 2 weeks.
- **Customization:** Feel free to add chopped nuts or a sprinkle of sea salt on top before baking for additional texture and flavor.

These Chocolate Fig Bars combine the sweet, chewy texture of figs with the rich, smooth taste of chocolate, creating a delightful treat that's perfect for any occasion.

Chocolate Almond Croissants

Ingredients:

For the Croissants:

- 1 package (14.1 oz) frozen puff pastry sheets (or 1 sheet, thawed)
- 1/2 cup almond paste (store-bought or homemade)
- 1/4 cup granulated sugar
- 1/4 cup unsalted butter, softened
- 1/2 cup semi-sweet chocolate chips or chopped dark chocolate
- 1 egg, beaten (for egg wash)
- 1/4 cup sliced almonds (for topping)

For the Almond Paste (Optional, if not using store-bought):

- 1 cup blanched almonds
- 1/2 cup powdered sugar
- 1/4 cup almond extract
- 1 tablespoon honey

Instructions:

1. **Prepare the Almond Paste (if making homemade):**
   - **Process Almonds:** In a food processor, process the blanched almonds until finely ground.
   - **Add Sugar:** Add the powdered sugar and pulse to combine.
   - **Add Extract and Honey:** Add the almond extract and honey. Process until the mixture forms a paste. If it's too dry, add a little water, one teaspoon at a time, until it reaches a spreadable consistency.
2. **Prepare the Puff Pastry:**
   - **Preheat Oven:** Preheat your oven to 375°F (190°C). Line a baking sheet with parchment paper.
   - **Roll Out Pastry:** Unfold the puff pastry sheet on a lightly floured surface. Roll it out slightly to smooth it out if needed.
3. **Assemble the Croissants:**
   - **Spread Almond Paste:** Spread a thin layer of almond paste over the puff pastry.
   - **Add Chocolate:** Sprinkle the semi-sweet chocolate chips evenly over the almond paste.
   - **Cut and Shape:** Cut the pastry into triangles or rectangles, depending on your desired croissant shape. For a classic croissant, roll up each triangle from the wide end to the tip, forming a crescent shape. For rectangles, fold or roll them as desired.
4. **Prepare for Baking:**
   - **Brush with Egg Wash:** Place the croissants on the prepared baking sheet. Brush each croissant with the beaten egg to give it a golden finish.
   - **Top with Almonds:** Sprinkle sliced almonds on top of each croissant.

5. **Bake the Croissants:**
   - **Bake:** Bake for 15-20 minutes, or until the croissants are puffed up, golden brown, and crispy.
6. **Cool and Serve:**
   - **Cool:** Allow the croissants to cool slightly on a wire rack before serving.

Tips:

- **Storage:** These croissants are best enjoyed fresh but can be stored in an airtight container at room temperature for up to 2 days. Reheat in the oven for a few minutes to crisp up.
- **Customization:** Feel free to add a dusting of powdered sugar or a drizzle of melted chocolate on top for an extra touch of sweetness.

These Chocolate Almond Croissants offer a perfect combination of flaky pastry, rich chocolate, and nutty almond flavor, making them a luxurious treat for breakfast or dessert.